The Central Business District

The Central
Business District

RAYMOND E. MURPHY, 1898 -

Clark University

ALDINE · ATHERTON
CHICAGO · NEW YORK

First published 1972 by
Aldine · Atherton, Inc.
529 South Wabash Avenue
Chicago, Illinois 60605

ISBN 0–202–10032–4
Library of Congress Catalog Number 76–159598

Printed in the United States of America

Preface

This book is a geographic study of the premier region of the city, the central business district. The author's contribution is not primarily research. Instead, for the most part he has summarized the work by which he and various others have added to our knowledge of the CBD. What were the objectives? The methods? The findings? The authors' maps and diagrams are included where they seem to help in answering these questions.

The central business district (the CBD) is first introduced, characterized briefly, and related to ideas of city structure and to central place theory. The problem of finding an objective method of delimiting CBDs is posed, and the central business index method of delimitation (the CBI technique) is explained in detail as it was developed in a nine-CBD study in the early 1950s. Then there is a summary of tentative generalizations that resulted from the project. In two chapters following, a number of studies of CBDs outside the United States are summarized.

After this series is a description and evaluation of the Census Bureau's CBD, a chapter that deals with the "core-frame" concept and other external relationships of the downtown, and a discussion of manufacturing and transportation in relation to the district. Then come two chapters that focus on the CBD in the process of change. One summarizes studies that deal with the CBD and the suburbs in competition over a period of several decades. The other temporal chapter focuses directly on CBDs changing through time.

In the concluding chapter of the book the future is the center of interest. The views of several writers known for their vigorous opinions regarding the CBD's prospects are summarized, and the influence of urban renewal on the CBD is discussed. Finally, the author attempts, through a consensus of these and his own ideas, to outline something of the probable future of the district.

The book is a recording in summary form of the efforts of a number of workers. Limitations are chiefly those of published CBD research. The

American downtown is emphasized, since that has been the author's focus in his own research. But some interesting CBD work has been carried on abroad, especially in South Africa, and the resulting studies play important roles in the book. Unfortunately, very little has been published on the CBDs of great American cities.

This work is intended for anyone interested in the urban scene. Though it may well be of interest to urban planners, it is not written particularly for them; it is aimed more at the general reader concerned with cities, and at the student. It is hoped that the student, if he is at all interested in urban affairs, can read the book with profit, and that it may inspire additional CBD research.

Though numerous footnote credits are indicated throughout the book, there is no attempt to list all these works in the bibliography. Instead, it is largely limited to sources that deal exclusively with the CBD.

The author's debt to the various people who have studied and written on the CBD is obvious, as, of course, is his special debt to J. E. Vance, Jr., who worked with him on the original research project that germinated this book. The author wishes to give credit, also, to Marion F. Murphy for her help at various stages of preparation of the book; to Jean M. Hunt, Lane J. Johnson, and Gerald J. Karaska for valuable comments and suggestions; and to William A. Koelsch for a particularly penetrating and helpful critical reading of the book in its semifinal stages.

Contents

The Central Business District

1

Introducing the CBD

The modern city as seen in American and other Western cultures is characterized by a variegated pattern of land-use areas. There are sections dominated by business establishments, localities where manufacturing prevails, vast expanses that are residential, and areas of vacant land awaiting development. Some of the land-use units are small and alternate one with another, but there are other considerable expanses where a single use predominates. The overall arrangement is not a random one; instead, a certain order prevails.

The use areas that are of substantial extent tend to be divided into distinctive subareas. There are various business districts, manufacturing concentrations, and residential neighborhoods. These subareas often have definite names, locations, and characteristics and are widely known throughout the city.

Generally, one of the subareas is better known than any of the others and has more characteristics that carry over from city to city. This is the *central business district* or *CBD,* often popularly known as *downtown.* The names "central business district," "central commercial district," "retail business section," "downtown business district," and several others have been used in place of "central business district," but this designation has become more and more predominant. "Downtown" is sometimes applied to the central city of a metropolitan area, but throughout this book it will be used only in the sense of being essentially synonymous with CBD. "Core" and "urban core" are used somewhat loosely either for the central city or for the CBD. And the British commonly use the term "central area" in place of CBD.

The prominence of the CBD is reflected in widespread familiarity with the area's name and location. Although the term "central business district" was not in common use a few decades ago, it is now part of the vocabulary of a surprising number of citizens; in fact, many people use the abbreviated designation, CBD, as is done throughout this book. They are likely to

1

know in a general way the location of the district in their city and to have a rough idea of its extent.

The nature of the CBD, the research by which it has been and is being investigated, the special possibilities of comparative CBD studies, and the enigma of the CBD's future constitute the major themes of this book.

Some Characteristics of the CBD

The CBD has no fence around it, no wall as there was around the city in Europe in the Middle Ages. You will never see a sign, "You are Entering the CBD," although there may be signs directing you to the city's downtown area. However, the district can be conceptualized and its position outlined on a map on the basis of this mental construct. How can this best be done? This is a question that will be answered at some length in later chapters.

Traditionally, the CBD has been thought of as a somewhat indefinite region of the city that nevertheless has certain distinctive characteristics. It is central, at least in terms of accessibility. It has a greater concentration of tall buildings than any other region of the city, since it normally includes most of the city's offices and largest retail stores. It is the area where vehicular and pedestrian traffic are likely to be most concentrated. It averages higher assessed land values and taxes paid than any other part of the city, and it draws its business from the whole urban area and from all ethnic groups and classes of people.

This is the CBD as we have come to know it. But the district is by no means static, nor was it so in the past. Until about half a century ago, the downtown was an area of multiple uses—residential, commercial, industrial, institutional. But, with the passage of time, overcrowding and obsolescence led first to the decline in residential use and later in manufacturing and wholesaling. Downtown land had become too valuable for these less intensive uses.

Today, although business (commercial) uses have been left in almost complete possession of the field, changes are still going on. Some types of establishments are declining while others tend to become more important. At the same time portions of the CBD are deteriorating while others are in the process of rejuvenation through urban renewal. One of the purposes of this book is to evaluate these changes and to speculate as to what they augur for the future.

One should not get the impression that the CBD typically displays a high degree of uniformity. Retail business uses and offices predominate, it is true, and give the district its primary character; but there are marked variations in the concentration of these activities within the CBD. From a point or area of maximum business activity and land values, there is, ordinarily, an uneven gradation outward toward an indefinite boundary. The edge of the district is more a zone than a line, and the fact that every CBD boundary is conceptual rather than real adds to the difficulties of CBD research.

The lack of complete uniformity is also reflected in a tendency toward regionalization of specific functions in the district in the form of financial areas, hotel sections, theater groupings, department store areas, night club concentrations, and other specialized localities. There is also a vertical zonation, normally with a concentration of the most active retailing at lower levels and offices higher up.

Despite the implication of its name, the CBD often is far from centrally located in its urban area. This is particularly likely to be true in the case of a port city, where a water body has interfered with the city's symmetrical development. But since normally the CBD is the urban area's chief focus of transportation it is the most accessible section of the city. In this sense it *is* central, even in the port case.

Related to the CBD's prime accessibility is a higher order of centrality than that possessed by any other business section of the urban area. This centrality means that, in addition to the presence of those activities found in lesser business areas of the city, the CBD is characterized by a concentration of establishments requiring ready accessibility to the entire tributary area.

As more and more people have come to realize that there is a CBD, the district has developed a dual reputation. It is, as has been pointed out, an area of superlatives, the very quintessence of urbanism, symbolic of the city and of city life. Prosperity or at least intensity of business activity seems almost implicit. On the other hand there is the undoubted problem character of the CBD. Rising land values and correspondingly increasing taxes have been plaguing the district. So, too, have the outlying shopping centers that have been springing up in nearly every urban area and cutting seriously into downtown business. Added to the high taxes of the CBD and the inroads of the shopping centers are the ever-increasing difficulties of access. In spite of general accessibility from various parts of the city there is likely to be serious crowding of the streets in and near the downtown as well as inadequate parking facilities. In view of these problems it is not surprising that the CBD has attracted much research attention from geographers, social scientists, and planners.

Theories of City Structure and the CBD

This preliminary assessment of the central business district obviously needs some theoretical foundation. How does the CBD fit into theories of structure that have been designed for the entire city? These theories are described here in general terms.

Half a century ago Ernest Burgess, a sociologist, suggested that the

American city might be viewed as consisting of five concentric zones, beginning with the city center.[1] They were (1) central business district, (2) zone in transition, (3) zone of workingmen's homes, (4) residential zone, (5) commuters' zone. Burgess considered particularly the evolution of the residential regions within a city. His scheme was devised with Chicago in mind, but many people agreed that in approximate terms such zones occurred in most cities at the time Burgess first advanced the theory. And there has been a tendency to regard the concept as applicable chiefly to growing commercial-industrial cities.

Since the central business district is the subject of this book, it is of interest to see how Burgess described the district in 1929: *"Zone II: The Central Business District.*—At the center of the city as the focus of its commercial, social, and civic life is situated the Central Business District. The heart of this district is the downtown retail district with its department stores, its smart shops, its office buildings, its clubs, its banks, its hotels, its theaters, its museums, and its headquarters of economic, social, civic, and political life."[2]

Implicit in Burgess' model was the idea that growth takes place by expansion along the broad margins of successive zones, for example, along the outer marginal belt of the CBD. But in many cities lateral growth of the CBD has slowed down or ceased within recent years. Moreover, Burgess' idea of marginal growth has been criticized on the basis of the widely observed tendency for growth along radial lines, following routeways that cut across the zones.

Homer Hoyt, a major critic of Burgess' zonal concept, provided an alternative theory that introduced two new elements: the effects of land pricing or rent and the influence of major transportation routes on the pattern of urban growth.[3] As a city grew, he said, competition for land at the center of the city resulted in land values so high that only business could afford the land, and the CBD resulted.

The rise in land values or rent gradually spreads from the center outward, according to Hoyt. But instead of the rise taking place along a broad circular front it occurs along main transportation routes. From empirical work on many cities, Hoyt further suggested that growth along any one of these routes tends to be characterized by similar types and quality of land use. The result is a star-shaped pattern of city growth with differing types and qualities of use radiating along different sectors toward the periphery of the city. Thus, a high-rent residential area in any quadrant will tend to

1. Ernest W. Burgess, "Urban Areas," in T. V. Smith and L. D. White, eds., *Chicago: An Experiment in Social Science Research* (Chicago: The University of Chicago Press, 1929), pp. 113–138.

2. Burgess, "Urban Areas," p. 114.

3. Homer Hoyt, *The Structure and Growth of Residential Neighborhoods in American Cities* (Washington, D.C.: U.S. Government Printing Office, 1939).

grow outward to the margin of the city in the same sector. Like the concentric zone theory, the sector theory gives scant attention to business land use and industry. The theory reflects best the development of residential areas.

Still a third idea is that of the role of multiple nuclei in city growth instead of growth around a single CBD core as in the concentric zone and sector theories. These nuclei may have existed from the time of origin of the city or developed as the growth of the city stimulated migration and specialization. The number of nuclei varies from city to city but the tendency is for them to be more numerous and specialized the larger the city. In a large city a number of nuclei may be identified; some of them are sub-nuclei within the CBD which is itself a nucleus. The financial district, theater district, hotel district, and other comparable developments are visible manifestations of the sub-nuclei in operation.

This "multiple nuclei concept," first suggested by R. D. McKenzie[4] but known especially through the work of C. D. Harris and E. L. Ullman,[5] is more flexible and less precise than Burgess' concentric zones and Hoyt's sectors. It does not produce a simple model of urban structure discernible in city after city. But it serves a useful purpose in calling attention to the fact that an urban area may have many centers and that new centers of activities or sub-nuclei may develop within existing nuclei. The theories of both Burgess and Hoyt imply the continued expansion of each land-use region around a single nucleus. The multiple nuclei idea provides an additional needed element in explaining details of the urban pattern.

All three concepts contribute to an understanding of the CBD. If you are downtown in a large city and are surrounded by great office buildings, department stores, banks, and variety stores, you may feel that surely what you see is living up to the idea of Burgess' central business district. In going outward from this prime business area, you are likely to find uses becoming more mixed, and an area of dense population and low-class housing may occur. You will have passed from the heart of the CBD into Burgess' zone in transition.

However, in this zone in transition you may well encounter an area of above-average quality development, extending out radially from the city's peak intersection along a major street. Better business buildings, better apartments, and, farther out, better single-family housing with more extensive grounds mark this as a high-quality sector following Hoyt's theory. There may be several sectors radiating out from the city center, varying in quality one from another but displaying considerable intra-sector uniform-

4. R. D. McKenzie, *The Metropolitan Community* (New York: McGraw-Hill Book Co., Inc., 1933) p. 198.

5. For further examples of the multiple nuclei concept see C. D. Harris and E. L. Ullman, "The Nature of Cities," *The Annals of the American Academy of Political and Social Science* 242 (November 1945): 13–15.

ity. This does not mean that the concentric zones are not represented, but, locally, they give way to wedges or sectors, each characterized by a consistently similar nature and quality of land use. Thus we may decide that both the Burgess and the Hoyt theories are represented.

In addition, the CBD itself may be thought of as one of the nuclei of the city. If the city is large enough, the CBD may have a hotel district, a theater district, etc., representing the effects of other nuclei or sub-nuclei within the CBD. In summary, the concentric zone and sector theories involve the CBD only as it relates to overall urban structure; but one can analyze the downtown, as well as the whole city, in terms of multiple nuclei.

Such theories of city structure are relevant to study of the CBD in only a limited way. Another concept, that of central-place, is more significant.

The CBD and Central-Place Theory

The rise of interest in central-place theory has been an important development in urban geography research in the last few decades. The concept will not be discussed at length here since it is adequately treated elsewhere in the literature[6] and since this book is intended chiefly as a study of a type of urban region, the CBD. Our concern is only with how and what central-place theory contributes to an understanding of the CBD.

Even for this purpose, however, a few words of introduction to the theory are necessary. Customarily, people ranked urban places in order of population. But some geographers and others asked if it wouldn't be more meaningful to consider the importance of these places for retail and service business and hence according to the people served and the areas over which this business service extended. Such a service ranking of the urban centers in an area may amount to a continuum, a continuous series with no natural breaks. But, according to central-place theory, such is not the case. Instead, there tends to be discrete groups of places with associated groups of functions. If this is so, it would give credence to the idea of grouping settlements into a system of distinct classes, the central-place hierarchy, with numerous minor settlements and a few major settlements. The theory also provides for a dispersed arrangement of settlement locations with correspondingly greater distances between important settlements.

How do these considerations affect our understanding of the CBD? The CBD is the specialized retail focus not only of the city but also of the region for which the city may be considered the central place. Outside the CBD but dispersed within the service area are subsidiary centers. The number and order of these subsidiaries are related to the order of the city as a central place and therefore to the order of its CBD.

6. For a listing of central place studies see Brian J. L. Berry and Allan Pred, *Central Place Studies: A Bibliography of Theory and Applications,* Bibliography Series, no. 1 (Philadelphia: Regional Science Research Institute, 1961); reprinted 1965 with supplement through 1964 by H. G. Barnum, R. Kasperson, and S. Kiuchi.

We may assume that the CBD of the chief urban center in an area will have to the highest degree the qualities listed earlier in this chapter: centrality, tall buildings, heavy vehicular and pedestrian traffic, high land values and taxes, and ability to draw business from a wide area and from all ethnic groups and classes of people. If one city has a higher central-place rank than a second city it follows that the CBD of the first will offer goods and services not available in the CBD of the second.

But central-place theory also applies on a different scale. There is a hierarchy of retail areas within cities. At this level the CBD is only one of the central places that can be recognized within an urban center. In the middle 1930s, Malcolm Proudfoot published a classification of retail structure of the city that illustrates this point.[7] His five types—central business district, outlying business center, principal business thoroughfare, neighborhood business street, and isolated store cluster—suggested in themselves a hierarchical arrangement within the city, although the linear, traffic-oriented categories are not strictly speaking central places.

Later, Hans Carol applied the central-place hierarchy idea to the city of Zurich, Switzerland.[8] He distinguished four levels: local business district (lowest order), neighborhood business district (low order), regional business district (middle order), and central business district (high order). Brian Berry, too, has recognized the basic central-place nature of the commercial pattern of the city's interior.[9]

Within the city, the CBD, as the central place of the highest order, functions at the highest level among these business areas. It is able to offer goods and services superior to those of any business area of lesser order. And, as the city's top-ranking central place, the CBD occupies the location of prime accessibility while other business centers are relegated to less advantageous locations. The CBD is characterized by a concentration of those establishments that need maximum accessibility to the entire city and its tributary area. Thus, it attracts specialized retailing, large-scale banking, advanced medical services, and other functions so unusual that people come from all parts of the urban area and even from smaller, neighboring cities to take advantage of them. In total, the CBD offers a much greater number and variety of goods and services than any other of the city's business areas.

Central-place theory enhances our understanding of city commercial structure by enlarging the foundations provided by the concentric zone, sector, and multiple nuclei theories. But it is both a more limited and a more refined expression. The three theories of city structure imply the prime cen-

7. Malcolm J. Proudfoot, "City Retail Structure," *Economic Geography* 13 (1937): 425–428.

8. Hans Carol, "The Hierarchy of Central Functions within the City," *Annals of the Association of American Geographers* 50 (1960): 419–438.

9. See, for example, Brian J. L. Berry, *Geography of Market Centers and Retail Distribution,* Foundations of Geography Series (Englewood Cliffs, N.J.: Prentice-Hall, Inc., 1967).

trality of the CBD but do not focus exclusively or even primarily upon commercial land use. Central-place theory, most closely related to the multiple nuclei theory, is directly concerned with commercial structure. From this vantage point, urban business structure can be thought of as a system consisting of one major and numerous lesser central places with accessory linear developments along important traffic arteries. Thus, central-place theory offers a framework within which to view the retail and service dominance and locational primacy of the CBD.

2

Preliminary Attempts at Delimitation

Since the CBD is an area, it would seem reasonable, as a first step in studying the CBD of any city, to outline it on a map. But where does it start? There is a critical point downtown that is likely to be well-known to the policeman on the beat and to the downtown businessman. This is the peak land-value intersection, or the PLVI.

The PLVI is the street intersection around which front-foot land values average highest. Variety stores (department stores, 5-and-10-cent stores, drug stores, cigar and news stores) are common in the vicinity, as are banks. Another telltale is the fact that pedestrians are most numerous here at the peak of the business day. From this point, various measures of commercial intensity tend to decline toward the edges of the city though this decline is sharper in some directions than in others. The area immediately around the peak point is important, too, and frequently is designated by such terms as "commercial core" and "hard core." And tongues of more than average commercial intensity are likely to extend outward along major traffic arteries. The PLVI is a convenient point of reference and will be referred to a number of times throughout this book.

Let us look further at the general area around the PLVI. In any city of substantial size, the peak point is likely to be surrounded by a built-up section of stores, banks, and offices. At the same time the whole assemblage is so central geographically or at least in terms of accessibility that it is easily recognized as part of the city's CBD. The PLVI and the area immediately surrounding it might be referred to as the "obvious CBD." But it is only the beginning; how far outward does the district extend?

The Boundary: Zone or Line?

This question brings us to the nature of the CBD boundary. You may have had the experience of being in the downtown area of a city, in a section that you could readily recognize as part of the city's obvious CBD. When you followed a street outward, the continuous business land use may have ended abruptly; there was a house or two and then a factory. This, you probably thought, must be the edge of the CBD. But just beyond came a cluster of a few stores and other business buildings. You realized then that the CBD boundary is not a definite one. It is gradational and fragmented, a zone rather than a line. A park or, in a state capital, a group of government buildings may locally result in a line boundary, but much more often the edge is a belt or zone.

This zonal nature of the CBD boundary has been noted by various students of the city. So also has an interesting characteristic of the zone: typically it is of low quality. Thus Walter Firey, writing in the early 1930s, referred to the edge of the central business district as "the blighted zone which generally lies between a city's central business district and the surrounding residential districts, . . ." p. 411)[1] and Robert Dickinson in 1946 spoke of the CBD boundary as a dingy-looking zone of deterioration. The supposed commercial potential of this border zone has resulted in artificially high land values, whereas in fact the zone in many cases has not been able to support prosperous commercial activities. Multifamily houses and rooming houses tend to be interspersed with marginal commercial establishments. Over the years it has been this zone that has furnished the sites for many of our urban renewal projects.

Firey also called attention to an interesting similarity between the edge of the CBD and the "rurban" (rural-urban) fringe which often surrounds a city (Fig. 2.1). Both, he claimed, are marginal areas between two types of land use—business and residences at the edge of the CBD, agriculture and residences in the rural-urban fringe. Both zones, he said, are areas of adjustment and friction, exhibiting to a high degree the dynamic qualities of the modern city. There is a tendency for slum conditions to occur in both.

How can the position of the border zone and hence of the CBD best be approximated on a map? Obviously, there is no exact way. Certainly, satisfactory results cannot be obtained through simple field observation: two people, walking outward from the city center and observing independently, would be unlikely to arrive at boundaries that corresponded at all closely.

Why An Exact Boundary Matters

Geographers, sociologists, economists, planners, and others have made studies, purportedly of CBDs, and have attempted in varying degrees to generalize from their results. But for each study, exactly what area was used? How was the boundary determined? And, it might be asked, why are such matters worth considering?

---

1. Walter Firey, "Ecological Considerations in Planning for Rurban Fringes," *American Sociological Review* 11 (1946): 411–423.

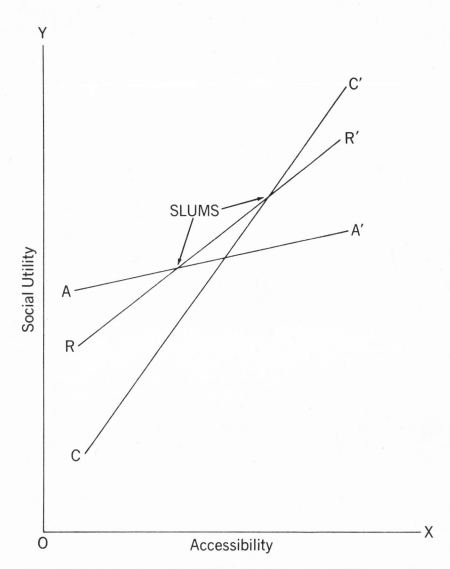

Note: AA′, agriculturally used land; RR′, residentially used land; CC′, commercially used land.

Source: Walter Firey, "Ecological Considerations in Planning for Rurban Fringes," *American Sociological Review* 11 (1946): Fig. 1.

Fig. 2.1. Amount of social utility yielded by specified land uses at varying degrees of accessibility to a population center

In the city planning office, such details may be of no great concern since the results of the CBD study being planned are generally intended for local use only. If, however, a geographer or other social scientist carries on his local research as a case study, hoping to draw inferences about CBDs in general, the matter of delimitation takes on more significance. And the method of delimiting the district is particularly critical when the research worker is making a study involving a number of cities and is trying, through comparisons of the several CBDs, to arrive at generalizations.

Throughout this book the words subjective and objective are used frequently. If the method of drawing a boundary is such that it results in a very different product depending upon who does the work, we would say the method is too subjective. In contrast, a method would be described as relatively objective if it is so definite that different individuals or groups using it would get essentially the same results. An objective delimitation method must be used if CBD comparisons are to be of real value.

A Research Inquiry Based on Nine Cities

With the paramount necessity for comparability in mind, James E. Vance, Jr., and the writer, in the early 1950s, undertook a CBD research project based on nine moderate-sized cities.[2] We hoped to find a satisfactory method of CBD delimitation (or to develop a reasonably objective method ourselves) and through its use in the nine cities to arrive at some tentative generalizations regarding the CBD. But first a general survey was made of methods that had been used or that might conceivably prove useful for delimiting the area.

Assuming a Boundary

As a first step, published research was considered that was in any sense geographic in nature and had focused on a central area either called the CBD or with what appeared to be CBD characteristics. There had been studies of that sort, some by geographers, of Nashville, Chicago, Madison, and other cities, and even some work by George Hartman in which a number of CBDs were compared as a basis for generalizations regarding CBD shape. But in none of these research studies purporting to deal with the CBD or its equivalent was any serious attempt made to develop or to use a definite method of CBD delimitation. In each case, the extent of the study area was just assumed or local opinions of its extent accepted.

A good example of the assuming of a boundary is found in a study of the Chicago CBD completed more than 30 years ago by Earl Johnson, a sociologist.[3] The study had a purpose and a method that would have done credit

2. Raymond E. Murphy and J. E. Vance, Jr., "Delimiting the CBD," *Economic Geography* 30 (1954): 189–222. See also Raymond E. Murphy and J. E. Vance, Jr., "A Comparative Study of Nine Central Business Districts," *Economic Geography* 30 (1954): 301–336, and Raymond E. Murphy, J. E. Vance, Jr., and Bart J. Epstein, "Internal Structure of the CBD," *Economic Geography* 31 (1955): 21–46.

3. Earl S. Johnson, *The Natural History of the Central Business District with Particular Reference to Chicago* (Ph.D. diss., University of Chicago, 1941). Available in microfilm.

to an urban geographer. Johnson summarized his objectives as, "to trace the sequence in the patterns of land use in Chicago's central business district from the days of earliest settlement to attainment by the community of metropolitan status." (pp. 2–3) His central hypothesis was: "For every type of economy which the community has represented there is a unique pattern of land use in the central business district; the two are not only temporarily co-existent but also causally related phenomena." (p. 37)

The area selected for study was

> bounded as follows: on the north by the main stream of the Chicago River; on the west by the south branch of the same river; on the south by Roosevelt Road (Twelfth Street); on the east from Roosevelt Road to Randolph Street by Michigan Avenue and from Randolph Street to the main stream of the river by Beaubien Court. Thus on two sides, the north and the west, its boundaries are provided by nature; on the south and east they are man-made. (p. 4)

The foregoing "constitutes by commonly accepted definition the central business district of the city" (p. 4) and is "generally recognized" as the central business district. Johnson went on to cite people and groups who had based their work on this boundary, and defended the area further on the grounds of spatial position—a complex of economic institutions is able to operate with optimal efficiency from this center. Apparently, in deciding upon the limits some attempt was made to follow ward boundaries.

Through Johnson's method of outlining the Chicago CBD seems to have been adequate for his study, it would not have served for comparing the Chicago CBD with that of some other city with the purpose of arriving at generalizations about CBDs. For this purpose, some standardized, reasonably objective delimitation technique would have been needed in order to outline really comparable areas.

Another example of assuming a CBD boundary is found in John Rannells' *The Core of the City: A Pilot Study of Changing Land Uses in Central Business Districts,* which is summarized later in this book. Much of Rannells' work is based on an area in central Philadelphia which he refers to as "The Philadelphia Central District." This is the " 'standard block' . . . which has been used for years by the city as a convenient map unit for recording data." (p. 86) Apparently, there has been no concern whatever with the desirability of outlining a CBD that could be objectively compared with delimited CBDs of other cities.

Local Official Usage as a Basis for Boundary

One obvious direction for the Murphy and Vance inquiry was to find out what delimitation methods were in use or had been used in various cities by official agencies. In most instances the planner sent a map showing the extent of the CBD of his city as it has been delimited locally and described the basis for the boundary, but there was little uniformity in methods. For some cities the zoning ordinance defined one CBD, the fire department used a different definition, and possibly the traffic ordinance still another. In most cities, though, a single CBD boundary was used, generally following city block lines. Rivers, railroad tracks, and the like were important factors in forming parts of the boundary, and a knowledge of local land use entered in.

But rarely was any attempt made to do the delimiting exactly. The area outlined was the one "generally understood locally" to be the CBD; in another instance the district's extent was arrived at "intuitively." Such delimitations obviously were highly subjective, with methods varying from city to city but adequate, apparently, for strictly local studies.

Perception Studies and CBD Delimitation

In recent years some people have advocated a more formal type of local opinion determination: perception studies. The perception idea is by no means new to geography but it is being given new emphasis. Concepts such as the CBD, these people say, cannot be exactly defined; the extent of the district in a city is fixed only by what people think. In accordance with this idea, maps of the central portion of the city are presented to various local people, such as men and women on the streets and clerks in the stores. Each person is asked to outline the CBD as he perceives it, and the results are averaged to arrive at a boundary.

The limits arrived at in this way are interesting since they reflect in a vague way the extent of the CBD as seen by the people of a particular city. But it hardly seems that local opinion thus casually arrived at can be counted upon to outline for different cities CBDs that are sufficiently comparable for worthwhile generalizations to result.

Later in this book the Census Bureau's method of outlining CBDs will be discussed. You will find that in a sense it too is based on perception, although it is perception by selected groups rather than by individuals.

Some Scandinavian Contributions to Delimitation Methodology

But more exact methods of delimitation are possible. Before much of this sort of research had begun in the United States, some Scandinavian geographers were trying ideas that are worth reviewing in an analysis of possible delimitation techniques.[4]

W. William-Olsson, for example, described a method used in analyzing the "central shopping district" of Stockholm.[5] Defining retail trade as trade

4. M. R. G. Conzen, "The Scandinavian Approach to Urban Geography," *Norsk Geografisk Tidskriff* 12 (1949): 86–91.
5. W. William-Olsson, "Stockholm: Its Structure and Development," *Geographical Review* 30 (1940): 420–438.

not only in goods but also in meals, amusements, and lodgings, he used the term "shop rent index" which he defined as the total of shop rents of a building divided by the length of the frontage of the building. This index he regarded as a numerical expression for shopping intensity of the structure. He presented this information graphically on maps of the Central Shopping District of Stockholm by means of rectangles, the base of each being a building frontage and the vertical, reaching away from the street, the shop rent index in kroner.

Two Norwegian geographers, studying dwelling and working places in Oslo, were unable to get shop rent data such as William-Olsson used for Stockholm, and hence used total trade instead.[6] Their "trade index" was plotted on a map in much the same manner as William-Olsson's shop rent index except that the vertical dimension of the rectangle was proportional to the value of total trade.

It might seem at first glance that some minimum shop rent index or trade index value could be used to mark the outer edge of the CBD of the American city. However, both methods require data that would be difficult if not impossible to assemble. And, for our purposes, the emphasis in both studies was too much upon shopping. According to the concept followed in this book, shopping is only part of the CBD story.

Volume of Trade and Delimitation

Volume of trade was used in the 1930s in a U. S. Census Bureau study that involved a CBD delimitation. It was a study of business areas in Philadelphia, supervised by Malcolm Proudfoot.[7] In setting up "intra-city business areas," "block-frontage-volume-of-sales" was used. This term refers to the total annual volume of sales, for each side of a block, of all stores fronting on that side. A normal block would have four such totals though the figure might be "O" for one or more sides if no establishments fronted on those sides. "For the outer zone of the central business district . . . a block frontage lower limit of $75,000 was used. . . ." (p. 7) An inner zone of the CBD also was delimited, with a block frontage lower limit of $300,000. Of course, if such a method were used today, the value data would be very different, but the idea is an interesting one.

In his study, Proudfoot used only volume of retail sales. This approach works better for outlying shopping centers than for the CBD, since in the CBD much business is carried on besides retail trade. In outlying shopping centers, retail trade characteristically is more predominant. Proudfoot, who was a Research Geographer for the Census Bureau when he super-

---

6. Tore Sund and Fridtjov Isachsen, *Bosteder og arbeidosteder i Oslo* (Oslo: Oslo kommune 1942).

7. U. S. Bureau of the Census, *Intra-City Business Census Statistics for Philadelphia, Pa.* Prepared under supervision of Malcolm J. Proudfoot, Research Geographer (May 1937).

vised this study, pointed out that for any city it would be possible to have the Census Bureau prepare at cost a map showing total volume not only of retail trade but of services and wholesale trade as well for each side of each block in the central portion of a city, and that these data could even be totaled by blocks if one preferred to work with whole blocks. But aside from the time and cost involved and certain restrictions on the use of such U. S. Census data, the method has other limitations. It fails to take account of offices, such as the central office of a large oil company; of banks; and of certain other activities that are important in the CBD. It is hard to see, too, how comparable volume-of-trade data could be obtained for such diverse establishments as stores, banks, and headquarters offices.

Building Heights

A possible measure for CBD delimitation that occurs to the casual observer almost instinctively is building heights. The CBD averages higher buildings than any other part of the city. No doubt you have had the experience of seeing a city in profile from a distance and have noted that the central portion generally towers above the rest of the city. The skyline of Chicago is particularly famous in this regard.

It would appear to follow that one should be able to use building heights as a basis for marking the edge of the CBD. This marking might be done on a lot basis, but lots are often irregular in size, and building heights rarely grade away evenly from the highest-value lots. The resulting boundary would be very irregular, almost impossible to approximate by a single line. A better plan might be to use building heights by blocks. A value for each block, representing the average height in stories, could be obtained by dividing total floor area at all levels in the block by the ground-floor area of the block. In this calculation, alleys are omitted.

In either case, however, whether by lots or by blocks, a building-heights map takes no account of land use. Factories, apartment houses, and other non-central business uses may rank with office buildings and department stores in terms of height. So building heights obviously have decided limitations in attempts to approximate CBD boundaries.

Distribution of Population and Delimitation

Use of population data, either directly or in terms of dwelling units, is another delimitation possibility to be considered. It is based on the fact that the CBD, according to any reasonable concept, is essentially lacking in permanent residents. Chief interest is in the central area of the city, where business land use tends to crowd out dwelling units. What residents there are in the CBD are likely to be concentrated in the outer fringe of the district.

Population totals, based of course on where people sleep, are available by census tracts, but the tract, which averages 50-60 blocks in size in some cities, is too large a unit for outlining a very precise area on the basis of population (see discussion of tracts in Chapter 7). And the average tract contains several thousand residents, far too many for defining an area that is supposed to be characterized by a virtual absence of residents. The Census Bureau also gives population by Census blocks, which are essentially regular city blocks. The block obviously is a better sized unit for CBD delimitation than the tract.

Two slightly differing types of population maps based on block data may be considered. A simple dot map of population, using block data, is one possibility. On a population dot map, the CBD would appear as an essentially blank area, bordered typically by a belt of dense population. The latter is the low-quality area that so commonly borders the district: the skid row, flophouse, tavern section. But at best the blank area is a very rough approximation of the CBD. And it is hard to fix an exact line on a dot map; we are looking for a more practicable boundary.

Block data can be used to produce a more objective map by dividing the population of each block by the block's area. The latter would have to be calculated, however, since block area data are not published. It might be possible to find a rational minimum density, to include in the CBD let us say only those contiguous blocks surrounding the PLVI that have less than a certain specified number of persons per thousand square feet.

But there is a serious objection to basing the extent of the CBD on absence of population, whether a simple population dot map or a block-density map is used, an objection similar to that raised regarding the use of building heights. Blank areas near the center of the map, though they may be due chiefly to the presence of central business activities, are subject to other explanations as well. Blocks of factories, parks, a large public school with its grounds would produce the same effect. Hence, use of the blank central area on either type of population map might give an exaggerated impression of the extent of the district.

Pattern of Employment and Delimitation

If it were possible to obtain data on the number of persons employed in offices, retail stores, and service establishments and to localize the information on a map, this might form the basis for a satisfactory CBD delimitation technique. Scandinavian geographers in their urban studies often have used such data to show various types of manufacturing and commercial establishments on maps. But for the Unites States such information is difficult to obtain. Though in most cities addresses and approximate employment totals are available for factories, similar information for commercial establishments are ordinarily unobtainable. To assemble this information would be too laborious a process for a reasonably rapid and objective delimitation technique.

Traffic Flow and Pedestrian Counts

Traffic flow and pedestrian counts, reflecting as they do the activity on the streets, suggest other possible approaches to CBD delimitation. They are sometimes used in establishing land values for commercial property. But our concern with them here is that the edge of the CBD on each street leading away from the PLVI might, conceivably, be fixed where certain minimum counts per unit of distance are recorded.

Traffic flow may be briefly dismissed since it has some very obvious flaws as a possible basis for a delimitation technique. Though in some cities through traffic is routed by way of the peak intersection, in others, fortunately an increasing number, the modern tendency is to route traffic so as to avoid this peak point, and to prohibit on-street parking in downtown areas during the busier hours of the day. Hence, traffic often bears little relation to volume of business in this centermost area of the city. And since cities have different policies in these matters, it is hard to see how traffic flow could furnish a reliable basis for delimiting comparable CBDs for different cities.

Pedestrian counts are considered somewhat more promising, since movements of people on the streets are essential to the functions that give real character to the CBD. Up-to-date pedestrian counts are rarely available for a city, at least in a form that would lend itself to CBD delimitation, but a field staff using counters and stationed at proper intervals can assemble the data without too much difficulty. Such counters are sometimes used where a company plans to establish a new store and wants to check customer potential. A minimum count per unit of distance would have to be agreed upon for fixing the edge of the CBD. The result would be a series of points, one on each major street reaching out from the center. These points could be connected in some way in order to outline a CBD. Since the absolute values worked with would differ from city to city, however, it might be found desirable to convert the values for each city into percentages of the highest pedestrian count value determined for that city, and to use a certain percentage as the CBD outer limit on each street. Here, too, of course, a CBD can then be outlined. The technique could be applied by blocks if desired, so that the resulting district would be a group of contiguous blocks rather than an amorphous area.

Such steps as those described appear to present no insurmountable difficulties. But the whole pedestrian-count method suffers from the same handicaps as those based on population density and building heights by blocks: the pedestrians may include workers coming or going from a relict factory or students from a downtown high school. In the case of pedestrian counts, however, such difficulties might be partially offset by proper timing of the counts so as to avoid these special non-central business pedestrian components. Properly timed air photos have been suggested.

Valuation Data as Basis for Delimitation

On an earlier page it was pointed out that the CBD averages higher in assessed land values and in taxes paid than any other part of the city. This is a matter of record. Though appraised values are considered superior, assessed values are more often available. That the high-land-value characteristic is more than conceptual is clear from any city map of assessed land values. A high-value area surrounds and extends out from the major downtown intersection; this area includes the CBD. Assuming this close relationship between land value and land use, how can assessed land-value data be used to outline the CBD of a city? And how can comparable CBDs for a number of cities be achieved on this basis?

For most cities, data on both land values and land and building values have been computed. Building values do not grade regularly from a peak point and besides they are constantly changing. Hence, land values are considered to present a greater potential for developing a CBD delimitation technique.

For the central part of the city, assessed land values commonly have been calculated on a front-foot basis. In computing the value of a particular lot or tract, adjustment factors are applied to take into account varying lot or tract depths and corner influences. This is done because the frontage on a street, particularly in business sections, is of considerably greater commercial value than the land farther to the rear of the lot. Thus the relative values of lots are more dependent upon their frontages on business streets than upon their sizes. To correct for unevenness in lot sizes, the front-foot values are commonly adjusted to a uniform 100-foot depth. Tables may be obtained to simplify this procedure.

It is true that, even when these data for the central portion of the city are plotted on a map, there still remains the problem of fixing the boundary line of the CBD. This amounts to a somewhat arbitrary judgment: a value is chosen that seems best to correspond to the edge of the CBD as its position has been inferred on other bases. In the 1950s, Charles Downe, the director of the Department of Planning of Worcester, Massachusetts, used assessed front-foot land values reduced to a uniform 100-foot depth in a CBD delimitation in that city. Using the plotted values and his experience from planning acitivites in Worcester, he decided to draw his CBD boundary at the outer limit of the lots with a value of $300 or more. He also delimited a "hard core," enclosing lots with front-foot land values of $2,000 or more. (Fig. 2.2.)

Of course, a technique of this sort invites questions regarding the reliability of assessment data. Apparently, even within a single city, there may be considerable variation in assessment practices. And, even if it is

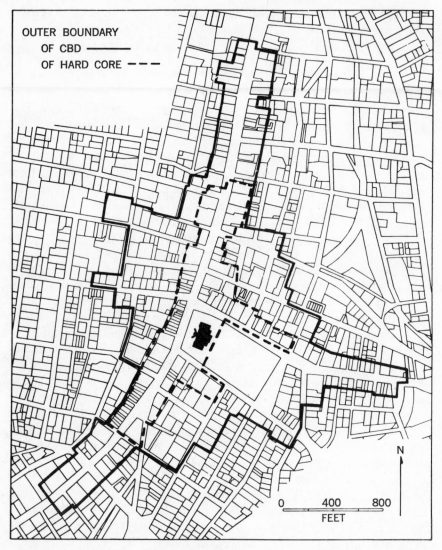

OUTER BOUNDARY
    OF CBD ————
    OF HARD CORE ― ― ―

N

0   400   800
          FEET

Note: The black area near the center of the map is the City Hall. The PLVI, though not indicated on the map, lies just northwest of the City Hall.
    Source: Raymond E. Murphy and J. E. Vance, Jr., "Delimiting the CBD," *Economic Geography*, 1954, Fig. 2.

Fig. 2.2. Worcester's CBD in the early 1950s as delimited by Charles Downe, Director of Worcester Department of Planning

assumed that the data for any one city are derived in a reasonably consistent manner, there are certainly great differences in such practices from city to city. Direct use of assessment data, therefore, could certainly not be expected to yield comparable CBDs for different cities. The $300 value limit used for the Worcester Central Business District might not have been suitable at all for delimiting the CBD of Milwaukee, or Seattle, or some other city which presumably had its own assessment practices.

It is possible that such difficulties could be overcome, however, through a system of percentages. The assessed value for the highest valued lot at 100-foot depth could be represented by the number 100; the value of each other lot could then be shown by the number corresponding to its percentage of the value of the peak lot; and a succession of lines could be drawn to show the decline in percentages away from the 100 per cent area. But there would still be the problem of deciding on the limiting value that should be used to mark the edge of the CBD. When the technique was applied to the CBDs of several cities, it was found that the lots with indexes of 5 per cent or more seemed best to represent the CBD (see Fig. 4.4). Such an index system could be applied, presumably, to the assessed lot values of each city and reasonably comparable CBDs for the various cities arrived at.

Land-value techniques require no land-use mapping, and the delimitation is a fine-textured one. But there are disadvantages inherent in any method based on land values. In some cities the data, though on the Assessor's books, have not been assembled; in others, for one reason or another, local authorities may be unwilling to make valuation information available. An additional difficulty is that tax-exempt property, such as, schools, churches, and public buildings, is commonly not assigned a valuation. With so many holes in the assessed values map, it is difficult to draw a smooth, continuous boundary.

There are at least two other objections to a land-value technique. If land valuation is done properly, it does not reflect the heights of buildings; yet, surely, this vertical dimension needs to be considered. And there is the shortcoming that the land-value technique shares with the delimitation methods discussed earlier: it does not discriminate among land uses. Thus, it is entirely possible for a factory block or a block of apartment buildings to occur in an area of high land values and hence, if land values are used, to be included in the CBD even though not central business in type. But this problem is not very likely to arise near the center of the CBD; it is near the edge that these other uses compete most successfully with central business for the land. And it is equally true that, along the edge of the CBD, central business uses may extend into areas of lower land values.

Land Use and Delimitation

Land values, though more promising than most of the other potential delimitation bases that have been discussed, are after all only a reflection of the uses to which land can be put. Why, then, should not land use itself furnish even more direct and realistic approaches to CBD delimitation? There are several possible methods which, though based on land use, do not require complete land-use mapping of the central portion of the city even on a reconnaissance basis. These will be considered first, leaving until later a method that is based on a reasonably complete land-use mapping of the central area of the city.

A Break in Continuity of Central Business Land Use

Perhaps the most obvious of all possibilities involves breaks in the continuity of central business land uses. Why not start in the downtown area that is unquestionably part of the CBD and walk outwards toward the edge of the city, closely observing the land use as you do? At some point on every street leading away from the PLVI the shops and offices and office buildings, occurring essentially without a break at first, will be found to give way to residences or factories or parks or some other use types that no one would seriously consider to be central business. It should be possible to plot a point of this sort on each of the streets that radiate or otherwise lead outward from the center.

The simplicity of the "break in continuity" idea makes it attractive, but actually it has decided limitations for outlining the CBD. How much of a break must there be for any significance to be attached to it? The decision would, unfortunately, be a highly subjective one in each case. How should the resulting points be connected on the map in order to yield a single, continuous area that we could call the CBD? Clearly, the whole procedure involves so much personal judgment that no two people would be likely to get very similar delimitations for a single city, and workers in various cities could hardly be expected to arrive by such means at CBDs that are at all comparable.

Types of Establishments Marking the Edge

Another simple observational method for CBD delimitation is based on the hypothesis that certain types of establishments, though rare in the CBD, tend to be concentrated at or near its boundary. Supermarkets, automobile sales rooms, filling stations, parking lots and parking garages, large furniture stores, and rooming houses are among the land-use types that have this reputation. To what degree do these establishments coincide with the boundary? Are they really concentrated at the CBD edge or is the CBD merely a relatively blank area on a map showing the distribution of any one of them?

In any case, edge establishments are far from a definite answer to the quest for a practicable method of CBD delimitation. Their chief possible value might be for a preliminary rough spotting of the boundary on the principal streets leading away from the city center.

Central Business Block Frontage

Another possible delimitation technique that does not require complete land-use mapping of the central portion of the city involves the use of street frontage profiles of the major streets around the peak land-value intersection. This mapping method was used by A. E. Parkins in a study of Nashville's "Retail Business Section" and described in a paper published in 1930.[8] It is something like the work of William-Olsson and that of Sund and Issachsen, discussed earlier in this chapter, except that in this case the vertical is divided into stories and the horizontal is divided into lots. Letters and numbers are used to indicate the individual types of establishments. Parkins focused on the major downtown business streets of Nashville but did not outline an area.

For delimiting the CBD, the uses could presumably be aggregated by blocks, and a block considered part of the CBD if it were one of a contiguous group around the PLVI and had a sufficiently high proportion of central business establishments. However, translations of the several profiles into a CBD in plan view would present obvious difficulties. The profiles furnish clues as to the general position of the CBD rather than themselves being an answer to our CBD delimitation problem.

Land-Use Mapping and CBD Delimitation

It is apparent that the land-use picture must be more broadly comprehended if land use is to form the basis for a reasonably practicable delimitation technique. The district is best thought of as an assemblage of land uses, some of which are especially distinctive. For analyzing the land uses in their areal arrangements, field mapping is an essential first step. Chapter 3 will illustrate the use of such field mapping in a recommended method of CBD delimitation.

8. A. E. Parkins, "Profiles of the Retail Business Section of Nashville, Tennessee, and their Interpretation," *Annals of the Association of American Geographers* 20 (1930): 164–175.

3

The Central Business Index Technique

In this chapter the Central Business Index or CBI method of CBD delimitation is presented. It is also known as the Murphy and Vance technique since it was developed by the author of this book in collaboration with J. E. Vance, Jr., in the research project referred to in Chapter 2. It requires land-use mapping of a substantial area, the land around the PLVI which is obviously CBD and an area extending far enough to encompass any other land that might conceivably fall within the district.

Several other considerations are involved. The technique requires a distinction between central business uses and land uses that are not central business in character though often found in downtown areas. The final calculations are by block and are based on the amount of space used for central business purposes compared with that for non-central business. Indexes are determined for each block, and the CBD is defined as consisting of those blocks that meet certain index values and are part of a contiguous group surrounding the PLVI, a group in which the individuals qualify according to rules which will be summarized later in this chapter. These are the major points in the delimitation method. Each phase of the technique will now be discussed in detail.

Central Business versus Non-Central Business Land Uses

Of course, not all of the land uses represented in the CBD are equally at home. The relict church, engulfed by CBD development but still active, the garment factory still clinging on in the fringe of the CBD, the wholesale house with trucks lined up at its loading platform, and the county court house each presents a very different picture in this respect from the department store, the general office building, and other establishments that obviously belong in the downtown retail assemblage. This distinction between non-central business and central business is fundamental to the technique of CBD delimitation here presented.

The really essential central business activities appear to be the retailing of goods and services and the performing of various financial and office functions. Stores of all sorts that retail merchandise, shops that offer services, banks and other financial institutions, and the whole miscellany of offices so typical of the center of a city are considered to be central business in character. Similar stores and shops and offices occur elsewhere in the city, but their area of maximum concentration normally is the CBD. These establishments are oriented around the PLVI and tend to serve the city as a whole rather than any one section or any one group of people. They are, moreover, able to accommodate themselves to limited space. Such establishments are the ones upon which delimitation of the district is based in the CBI method.

In contrast, various types of land use, though occurring sometimes in the CBD, are not considered to be central business in character. Wholesaling (with stocks) is one of these.[1] Located more by the presence of railroads and major highway routes through the city than by the pull of centrality, it is not primarily a central business function. Even more obviously, factories and residential units (private dwellings, apartment houses, and rooming houses) though occasionally occurring in the CBD are out of place there.

Absence of the normal profit motive excludes from the central business list churches and other religious establishments, public and other non-profit making schools, municipal and other government buildings, parks, organizational establishments such as the quarters of fraternal orders, and several other types of space occupance. Establishments included in this group perform useful functions, of course, and they result indirectly in additional business. In some cities they add distinction and charm to the district. There may be a common or a central park, a public garden, an architecturally distinguished city hall, a church spire or two, or the state capitol. But these are, after all, exceptions. In the average CBD such nonconforming uses are lost in a sea of business. They add to the crowding and hence to the problems of the CBD without having the qualities that give the area its most essential character.

It might be argued that certain forms of retailing, though occurring in the CBD, are non-central business in nature. Certainly, supermarkets, filling stations, and automobile sales agencies are rare within the CBD of

---

1. Wholesaling without stocks is normally considered an office function and is so treated throughout this book. The wholesaling shown in the list of page 26 and in Appendix C is wholesaling with stocks. In this connection see the Alderson and Sessions classification in Chapter 11 of this book; see also J. E. Vance, Jr., *The Merchant's World: the Geography of Wholesaling* (Englewood Cliffs, N.J.: Prentice-Hall, Inc., 1970), pp. 45 and 133.

a city of substantial size. But if these specific types of retailing are non-central business, there are others that are only a little less so. And, although wholesaling with stocks is considered non-central business, there are certain types of such wholesaling that profit considerably from a central location within the city and even limited types of manufacturing that are attracted to the downtown. If we had to split retailing on the basis of degree of centrality required, we would be faced with the necessity for making a whole series of centrality judgments that are unnecessary for the simple technique of CBD delimitation presented here. Hence, in the method being described, all retailing is classified as central business and all wholesaling and manufacturing as non-certral business.

An exception to the general rule regarding the non-central business classification of manufacturing is made in the case of a city newspaper. Since the same concern often sells advertising in the newspaper, prints the paper, and retails it, the whole operation is closely identified with other central business activities. Newspapers, therefore, are considered part of the central business assemblage, along with stores retailing ordinary merchandise, shops offering services, and the miscellany of offices, even though the getting out of a newspaper does have many of the aspects of manufacturing.

A problem is presented, too, by large, specialized office buildings such as the home or regional office of an insurance agency, an oil company, a telephone company, a steamship line, or a railroad. Often they might be located equally well almost anywhere in the city. But they are similar in type to other CBD offices, and they undoubtedly derive benefits from association with places such as banks, lawyers' offices, hotels, and restaurants, that do belong in the district. Hence, they are included in the group of central business establishments.

In any CBD, most of the land uses are unquestionably central business in character, but others, though occurring to some extent, are better classified as non-central business. These general types of land occupance considered to be non-central business in character are the following:

1. Permanent residences (including apartment buildings and rooming houses)
2. Government and public property (including parks and public schools as well as establishments carrying out city, county, state, and federal government functions)
3. Organizational establishments (churches, fraternal orders, colleges, etc.)
4. Industrial establishments (except newspapers)
5. Wholesaling with stocks, and commercial storage
6. Vacant buildings or empty stores
7. Vacant lots
8. Railroad tracks and switching yards

All of them are found to some degree in CBDs, but they are considered to be either antagonistic to true central business uses, as is the case with permanent residences and industrial establishments, or neutral, typified by government land use and occasional non-central business uses that may variously add to the attractiveness of the downtown. In either event they contribute little to the interplay of retail activities that characterizes the CBD. The distinction between these non-central business uses and central business uses is fundamental to the delimitation method being presented here.

The Mapping Procedure

Outlining of the CBD is best based on field mapping of land use. The area to be mapped was designated at the beginning of this chapter: the land around the PLVI that might be called the obvious CBD and also a belt sufficiently wide to include any land that might conceivably fall within the district. In this mapping, due consideration must be given to upper stories. The CBD involves three dimensions. Any measures of intensity of land use in the district must take the vertical dimension into account. The land use of upper stories is a part of the CBD picture just as is that of the ground floor.

In carrying out the mapping of CBD delimitation, a lot-line map on a scale of 1 inch to 200 feet has been found best. A scale of 1 inch to 100 feet or larger adds considerably to the labor of measuring the spaces on the map; at a scale of less than 1 inch to 200 feet, it is difficult to show sufficient detail. Fortunately, however, a base map at the 1 inch to 200 feet scale, showing lot lines, normally is obtainable from the planning board or some other city agency, or can be obtained by enlarging or reducing a map that is available.

The end products of the mapping are three land-use maps of the entire central portion of the city: one for the ground floor, one for the second floor, and an upper-floors map that represents a generalization of the land use of the third and higher floors.

In some CBDs, many basements house independent central business units: there are grocery stores, restaurants, shoeshine parlors, bookstores, and the like. But such basement stores and shops generally occur only intermittently. They would be difficult to take account of in field mapping such as that on which this delimitation technique is based, and can be disregarded if only a delimitation of the district as a whole is desired. But if a complete inventory of floor space in the CBD is being attempted, basement use should be included. Unquestionably, the extent and nature of CBD basement use would make an intriguing topic for investigation.

When the purpose of the land-use mapping is merely to delimit the CBD, it is sufficient simply to divide all the land use into central business uses and non-central business uses. These may be designated on the map by the letters "C" and "X" respectively. In order to make the method clear, the details are shown for a block of downtown Tulsa as of about 1950 (Fig. 3.1 with Table 3.1). Section I shows a plan view of the block. Section II shows profiles.

Profiling has been found to be a useful method of recording land-use information in the field where most of the buildings are several stories in height. It is recommended for CBD mapping of cities of 100,000 or more or at least in mapping their built-up portions. The profiles are constructed on ordinary lined tablets. The horizontal scale is the same as the scale of the base map, and the space between each two lines on the tablet is considered to be one story. On these profiles each non-central business unit for each floor is indicated by an "X"; each other space unit is marked with the letter "C," which indicates the presence of a central business use. Although the profiles shown are for the four sides of one block, normal practice in the field is to construct the profile for the same side of a street for a series of blocks. Other streets are similarly profiled, and the information thus accumulated is transferred in the office to first, second, and upper-floors maps of the area under consideration.

With a smaller city there may be few buildings over three stories high. In that case profiles are hardly necessary. Instead, maps of each of the three levels can be constructed in the field, using a fractional code. Where only one floor is represented, a simple "C" or "X" will suffice for each land-use unit; if two floors, a two-letter fraction may be necessary, representing land use on the ground floor first, and, above it, land use on the second floor. Of course there might be one or two tall buildings, even in such a small city. If there were, for example, a five-story building with a store at street level of the space unit being considered, an office on the second floor, and three floors of apartments above, the situation would be shown by a "C" with a line above it, then another "C" above that with a line above, and then "X(3)." The three final maps would look just as they would if profiles had been used.

Section III of Figure 3.1 shows the three land-use maps of the Tulsa block that would result from normal mapping procedure. They are the end products of the mapping regardless of the details of the method used. Sometimes the land uses do not correspond exactly to lot lines, though the lot lines are useful as guides. In the case of the block shown, the ground-floor map departs considerably from the original lot lines. For example, the lot at the corner of Fourth Street and Detroit Avenue is divided among seven establishments or uses.

It may make the picture clearer to say that every areal unit of land use is considered to be one story in vertical dimension. A parking lot (either "customer" or "commercial" in type) is mapped as one story of "C," and a vacant lot as one story of "X." Moreover, each building is mapped as if it occupied its entire lot unless departures from this situation are extreme.

Where the second floor or upper floors of use occupy substantially less than the total area of a lot, however, an attempt is made to record the facts so as to approximate the true extent of the buildings at these higher levels.

The third- or upper-floors map is a generalized representation of utilization at the third and higher floors. Above the second floor, use is normally so uniform that such a generalization is practicable. On the upper-floors map a letter standing alone represents third-floor use only, unless a number is given. If there are more than three stories then a number is shown. This tells how many floors are assumed to have approximately the same use as that indicated for the third floor. Thus, on the upper-floors map of Figure 3.1 the letter "X" standing alone shows that the building at the corner of Cincinnati Avenue and Fourth Street is three stories high with the top floor in non-central business uses. And the letter "C" accompanied by the number "5" indicates that, at the corner of Cincinnati Avenue and Fifth Street, central business uses predominate on the third to seventh floors of a seven-story building.

Of course, it is possible for sharp differences in floor space use to exist above the third floor. If these are substantial and obvious, they should be taken into account. Suppose, for example, a department store occupies the lower three floors of a five-story building and that the upper two floors of the building are used by a fraternal organization or by apartments. The simplest way to indicate this on the map would be to show on the upper-floors map approximately one-third of the space as "C(3)" and two-thirds as "X(3)." In this connection it should be remembered that the three maps are not made to show exact patterns of central business and non-central business establishments on each floor but merely to form the basis for calculations leading to delimitation of the CBD, and it should be kept in mind that the whole method is reconnaissance in nature. Great detail in mapping would defeat the purpose of the technique through greatly adding to the mapping time. Thus, the use of the third and higher floors can normally be determined adequately by looking upward from across the street or, at most, by consulting a front hall directory.

Although a single block is used here in order to make the method of profiling and map construction clear, in practice the profile may be made for the same side of a street for a series of blocks. And the end product is not a number of maps of individual blocks but three maps (ground floor, second floor, and upper floors) for the entire central portion of the city. Of course, for a city considerably larger than the ones worked with in the nine-city study, each map might have to be presented in several sections.

In applying the CBI method, some detail is shown regarding one group of non-central business uses, government establishments, although none chanced to occur in the block shown in Figure 3.1. They are indicated with the "X" designation just as are other non-central business establishments, but they are also labeled in some manner on the maps. This is done

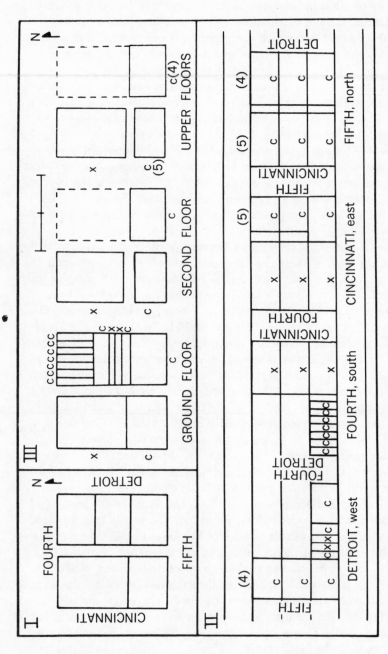

Note: A plan view of the block showing lot lines (I) is followed by profiles (II) and the three resulting land-use maps (III). Each profile is drawn from left to right as the observer faces the block. "DETROIT, west" refers to the west side of Detroit Avenue; "FOURTH, south," to the south side of Fourth Street; and so on around the block.

Source: Raymond E. Murphy and J. E. Vance, Jr., "Delimiting the CBD," *Economic Geography*, 1954, Fig. 5.

Fig. 3.1. A block of downtown Tulsa

Table 3.1. *Measurements and calculations for Tulsa block shown in Figure 3.1*

First Floor		Second Floor		Upper Floors			Block Inventory	
Use	Space	Use	Space	Use	Space	Adjusted Value	Use	Space
C	0.350	C	0.350	C	0.350 x 4	1.400	C	4.935
C	0.385	C	0.315	C	0.315 x 5	1.575	X	2.135
X	0.665	X	0.665	X	0.665	0.665	Total	7.070
C	0.050							
C	0.050							
C	0.050							
C	0.050							
C	0.050							
C	0.050							
C	0.050							
C	0.140							
X	0.070							
X	0.070							
C	0.070							
Total	2.100	Total	1.330			3.640	Total Space =	7.070

Central Business Height Index = "C" space ÷ Ground Floor Area = 4.935 ÷ 2.100 = 2.4.

Central Business Intensity Index = ("C" space ÷ Total Space) x 100 = (4.935 ÷ 7.070) x 100 = 69.8%.

Note: Measurements begin with first land use at southwest corner of block and proceed clockwise around block. Measurements are in square inches at a scale of 1 inch to 200 feet, but in reproduction Figure 3.1 was reduced to 80 per cent of its original size. Therefore, measurements made from it must be increased by one-fifth to equal the numbers shown in this table.

Source: Murphy and Vance, "Delimiting the CBD," *Economic Geography* 30 (1954).

because in using the method a special rule is applied to some governmental structures. This and other special rules for applying the technique are listed later in this chapter.

The immediately preceding pages deal with the situation where the purpose of the study is to delimit a CBD that will be comparable with other CBDs similarly delimited. For this purpose it is sufficient to classify all land uses as "C" (central business) or "X" (non-central business.) However, it is entirely possible in the mapping, instead of just using "C" and "X", to use a detailed breakdown of land uses. Professor Vance and the author used such a breakdown in the study of the nine CBDs in which the CBI method of delimitation was developed. Letter combinations and colors were used in the field. The data collected formed the basis for some of the generalizations that will be discussed in Chapter 4. (For the terminology used in the detailed land-use classification of the nine-CBD project, see Appendix C of this book.) The same detail can be carried through the measurements described on the following pages. Eventually, however, each item is listed under "C" or under "X" and the extent of the delimited district is exactly the same as if the simpler mapping procedure had been used.

Special problems are faced in delimiting the CBD where urban renewal is under way. Such projects are fairly common in the outer portions of CBDs. The difficulty arises because some of the plans for these areas are still in a semifinal stage. Normally, the probable uses can be determined sufficiently to tell whether each block is or will be part of the CBD. But for a block or two a careful study of plans and even some educated guesses may be necessary. For these blocks an inventory of exact space uses such as that mentioned in the preceding paragraph may prove impossible.

Office Calculations

The office calculations that follow involve finding from the three maps the total floor area, the ground-floor area, and the central business floor area for each block of the section being considered. Though the information is recorded by lots, it is aggregated by blocks, and the CBD is made up of block units. Here, one may ask, why use blocks? Why not lots? Or why not split blocks where they are very large or awkward in shape?

The use of lots would give a finer-textured delimitation than can be achieved with blocks, and splitting blocks would have somewhat the same effect. A finer texture might seem desirable, but lots are so small that a highly irregular effect would result from their use so that the drawing of a single-line boundary would become virtually impossible. At best the process would be far from objective, and blocks vary so much in size and shape within cities and from city to city that any attempt to split blocks would have the same non-objective effect. There is another argument against using lots or splitting blocks. Such procedures imply a high degree of precision whereas the whole CBI method is admittedly an approximate one. For these reasons all calculations are summed up by blocks rather than by smaller units and the CBD is considered to be a group of contiguous blocks.

It is sometimes hard to decide just what constitutes a block. Perhaps the best solution to this problem is to consider that a block ends only where a named street occurs. This is a rule that works in most American cities but which occasionally may give trouble because of local quirks in terminology. Probably the best answer is to adhere to the "named street" principle where this is at all possible but to be prepared to adjust to fit local circumstances, always keeping in mind the necessity of comparability from city to city.

All measurements on the three land-use maps are based on floor areas, but, since an assumption of equal height is made for all floors, the height factor is omitted from the calculations. A pattern of squares .1 inch on a side ruled on transparent paper or on tracing linen is recommended for carrying out the measurements. A vacant lot or a parking lot is considered to be one floor in height, like a one-story building, so the total ground-floor space in the block is the total ground-floor area minus alleys. Second-floor space is the total floor area at the second-floor level of all buildings in the block; and upper-floor space is the total of all floor areas at all levels above the second. The system of tabulating the data from the area computations should be clear from Figure 3.1 and Table 3.1. Measurements begin at the southeast corner of the block and proceed clockwise around the block. This regularity of procedure simplifies any later checking that may become necessary.

Two Critical Ratios

The next step involves the calculation of two critical ratios for each of the blocks included in the area mapped. The first of these, Central Business Height Index (CBHI), is the number of floors of central business uses if these are thought of as spread evenly over the block. It is obtained by dividing the total floor area of central business uses in the block at all levels (the "C" space) by the total ground-floor area (CBHI = central business space ÷ total ground-floor area). The second ratio, Central Business Intensity Index (CBII), is the proportion of all floor space in the block that is in central business uses. It is the percentage that floor area in central business uses at all levels (the "C" space) makes up of the total floor space at all levels (CBII = [central business space ÷ total floor space] x 100). In summary, note that the Tulsa block shown in Figure 3.1 has a CBHI of 2.4 and a CBII of 69.8 per cent.

It may be wondered why two indexes were considered necessary. Why would it not be sufficient simply to include in the CBD those blocks with CBHIs of 1 or more? A block might, for instance, have a CBHI of 2. This would mean that floor space used for central business totaled the equivalent of a two-story building covering the entire block. Certainly this should qualify the block adequately for the CBD.

But the CBHI fails to show the proportion of space in central business uses. Though the CBHI is 2 for the block just mentioned, this value could result from the entire block being occupied by two stories of central business uses overlain by four stories of apartments or four stories of manufacturing, and it would seem inappropriate to include in the CBD a block in which more space is used for non-central business than for central business uses. Requiring the block to meet the 50 per cent CBII minimum in addition to the prescribed CBHI value overcomes this difficulty, since it means that at least half of all the floor space in the block is in central business uses.

On the other hand a delimitation based on the CBII alone has this fault: it takes no account of the gross amount of central business floor space. A block might have a CBII of 50 per cent, which would appear to place it within the CBD, but this might be achieved by a one-story building that, though entirely devoted to central business uses, occupied only half of an otherwise vacant block. Certainly, such a block would not qualify. So the CBII alone also is unsatisfactory; it was decided that to be eligible for the CBD a block should satisfy both indexes.

Of course, indexes such as these have no inherently critical levels. To a considerable extent, such limiting values have to be based upon reasoning supported by experience from numerous field observations. In the research project on which the CBI method was based, it was decided, after a great deal of field checking, that to be included in the district a block should have a CBHI of at least 1; that is, the total space in the block devoted to central business uses should be equivalent at least to a one-story building covering the entire block. Through a similar combination of reasoning and field observations, it was decided that the CBII must have a value of 50 per cent or more to be included in the CBD. That is, central business had to occupy 50 per cent or more of the total floor space at all levels.

The Method in Detail

The CBI method for delimiting the CBD may now be stated in full. It involves the CBHI, the CBII, the PLVI, and also requires the application of certain rules. The method may be summed up as follows, essentially as worded by Vance and the author in our original delimitation study:

1. To be considered part of the CBD, a block must have a CBHI of 1 or more and a CBII of 50 per cent or more, and it must be one of a contiguous group of blocks surrounding the PLVI that meet these index requirements. Even though a block touches another only at one corner they are considered to be contiguous.

2. A block that does not reach the required index values but is surrounded by blocks that do is considered part of the CBD.

3. A block completely occupied by the buildings and grounds of a city hall or other municipal office building, a municipal auditorium, city police or fire department headquarters, or a central post office is included within the CBD if it is adjacent to (or contiguous with) blocks meeting the standard requirements. In some cities it will be necessary to add to this list the buildings and grounds of certain other government establishments: the courthouse in a county seat, the capitol building of a state capital, and occasionally certain Federal buildings in addition to the post office, e.g., a Federal court building or other Federal office building the activities of which are closely integrated with those of the city and its region. In no instance should such government buildings as those described in this paragraph result in the extension of the CBD for more than one block beyond normal CBD blocks. And a group of such government buildings cannot be split. Thus where there is a cluster of state buildings occupying several blocks that border the CBD, as in some state capitals, the whole group is considered to lie outside the CBD.

4. If the structures mentioned in Rule 3 occupy only part of a block which is contiguous with normal CBD blocks and if the inclusion of these establishments as central business would bring the two indexes of the block to the required totals, then the block is considered part of the CBD.

5. Blocks located beyond railroad tracks or beyond a freeway are not considered contiguous to the main body of CBD blocks unless the tracks and freeway are so completely underground (or overhead) as to allow free access to the main mass of CBD blocks.

The CBD of Worcester, Massachusetts

The method described can be better understood when applied to specific CBDs. Take, for example, the CBD of Worcester, Massachusetts, a city which had a population of 186,587 within its corporate limits at the time of the 1960 Census. Detailed mapping in the early 1950s yielded ratio values for some 40 or 50 blocks in central Worcester (Fig. 3.2). In the area mapped, a number of blocks met both the index values, and a few others satisfied one index but not the other. It might seem that the blocks in central Worcester which qualified on both indexes would automatically have made up the CBD. But it isn't as simple as that. It should be remembered that certain rules are part of the definition.

Consider how these rules affected the problem of outlining the Worcester CBD. Worcester's CBD is elongated in a roughly north–south direction along its axis, Main Street. Relatively steep slopes to the west, particularly north of the center, and the presence of railroad tracks to the east help to account for this shape. The delimitation problem in Worcester is complicated by a great range of block sizes. A block south of the district and a cluster of three small blocks east of it, all four readily distinguishable on the map, though they satisfied both indexes, were omitted from the

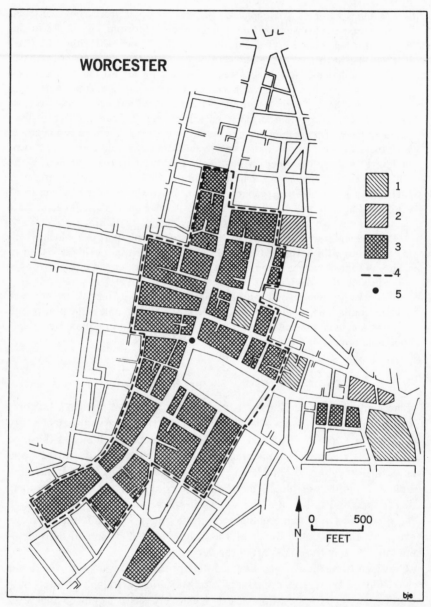

Key to legend: 1. Central Business Height Index of 1 or more; 2. Central Business Intensity Index of 50 or more; 3. Central Business Height Index of 1 or more and Central Business Intensity Index of 50 or more; 4. CBD boundary; 5. PLVI.

Source: Raymond E. Murphy and J. E. Vance, Jr., "Delimiting the CBD," *Economic Geography*, 1954, Fig. 6.

Fig. 3.2. Worcester's CBD

CBD because they were not contiguous to the main group of blocks around the PLVI, the point where Pleasant Street reaches Main from the west and continues southeastward as Front Street. Special cases of included blocks that did not reach the required index levels were the small post office block, in the southern portion of the district; the elongated block occupied by the city hall and the common just southeast of the PLVI; and, farther north, two blocks that were essentially surrounded by blocks with the specified index values. A county courthouse and a municipal building, located approximately a city block north of the district, were automatically excluded because they were separated from the main CBD by several blocks that did not reach either of the required index values.

The Tulsa CBD

Land-use mapping of downtown Tulsa was carried out at about the same time as the work in Worcester, but the picture presented by the Tulsa district was much simpler (Fig. 3.3). Tulsa's CBD has a rolling site. The PLVI, at the crossing of Fourth Street (trending ENE–WSW) and Main Street, is on a minor rise of land from which there is a slope outward in all directions. Railroad tracks occur at the northern edge of the district and also just to the east of the CBD. The only irregularity was a block at the northwest corner of the district, partly occupied by the central post office. It was included in the CBD under Rule 4.

Evaluation of the CBI Method

It seems desirable, at this point, to look back over the CBI method of delimitation. What are its shortcomings? Its good points?

First of all, it should be emphasized that the boundary which results from application of the method in any city is not *the* boundary of *the* CBD of that city. To claim that it is would indeed be naive, since, as pointed out earlier, the CBD is a concept, not a reality. Moreover, the edge of the CBD is unquestionably a zone and our boundary is a line. But the area delimited probably does include most of the CBD of the city, and the boundary is believed to be as fair an approximation of the zonal boundary as any single line could be. Since in each city in which the method is applied the boundary is drawn according to the same indexes and the same rules, the areas delimited in the various cities should be reasonably comparable. But the model is empirical rather than genetic; it is advanced more as a tool for studying the city than as having any significant implications as to the CBD's origin.

The method has certain obvious shortcomings. For instance, the delimitation is by block units; and block shape and block size differ from city to

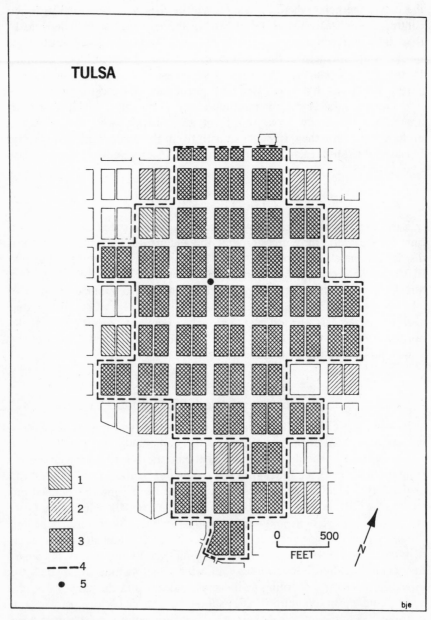

TULSA

Key to legend: 1. Central Business Height Index of 1 or more; 2. Central Business Intensity Index of 50 or more; 3. Central Business Height Index of 1 or more and Central Business Intensity Index of 50 or more; 4. CBD boundary; 5. PLVI.

Source: Raymond E. Murphy and J. E. Vance, Jr., "Delimiting the CBD," *Economic Geography*, 1954, Fig. 12.

Fig. 3.3. Tulsa's CBD

city and even within cities. Long, narrow blocks make application of the technique difficult, and where there is a great range in block sizes within the city results are likely not to be very reliable. But census tracts were considered far too large for any reasonably fine-textured delimitation.

The indexes were based upon a subjective classification of certain establishments as central business and others as non-central business. It is hardly to be expected that everyone will agree with the decisions involved in this twofold classification. For example, it has been argued by some that the central post office, the city hall, and even the courthouse in a county seat city should be considered to represent central businesses. But are they fundamentally different from other government buildings? Lack of the normal profit motive sets them apart from ordinary central business activities. They are taken into account in the CBI method through a special rule, but perhaps they should have been included in the central business list.

Another point that might be debated is how to treat commercial parking. In the nine-city study, commercial parking lots were considered as one floor of central business use, but admittedly they do not represent a very intensive commercial use. Perhaps a commercial parking lot should be considered the equivalent of only half a floor of other central business uses.

There is also a factor of quality which the method fails to take into account. Thus, there may be two blocks with identical indexes but one may be characterized by much lower grade establishments than the other. This is well illustrated by hotels. A ten-story hotel may be the best hotel in the city or it may be of obviously low quality. A jewelry store may handle an exclusive line of goods but another with the same land-use classification may be on the lower edge of respectability. Perhaps differences such as these should be considered in delimiting the CBD, but it is difficult to measure quality objectively.

It must be remembered, too, that the method was based on cities of a limited size range (see Appendix B). Will it work for a city of 25,000? Attempts to apply it to cities of this size and smaller have revealed serious limitations. In such a small city only a few blocks could possibly meet the required index values, and the inclusion or exclusion of a single block would mean a considerable percentage difference in the size of the CBD. The factor of block shape, too, is more serious in small cities. If the blocks are long and narrow, extending at right angles back from the main street into a residential area, the indexes may not quite reach the values necessary for inclusion of the blocks in the CBD. Most of the main business area may be excluded. In fact it seems very doubtful if such a small place has a CBD at all in the same terms as that of a city of 100,000 or more.

No information is available as to the applicability of the CBI method to very large cities. No doubt it has been used in some cases, but there is a tendency in such a city for people using the method to adapt it to their own city's needs, which of course means that comparability with other cities is lost. It seems possible, however, that in very large cities the technique might serve to identify not only the CBD itself but major secondary business districts as well. For the latter purpose, of course, one would have to outline clusters separated from the group centered at the PLVI. But a thorough testing of the method and its concomitants in very large cities remains to be carried out.

Balanced against the shortcomings of the CBI method is the fact that the delimitation is realistic and works well except in very small and possibly very large cities. It can be carried out rapidly. In fact, after some experience, it is possible for the field man to determine almost at a glance the blocks that will unquestionably meet the index and contiguity requirements for belonging to the CBD and those that unquestionably will not, leaving only a fringe of doubtful blocks for closer study. Figure 3.4 shows the approximate extent of the Providence CBD as determined in several hours in the field. Such a preliminary reconnaissance can be carried out in a small fraction of the time needed for applying the CBI method in full. The large dot on the map marks the PLVI. Each block that clearly met the CBHI and the CBII and also the contiguity requirements is marked with a "C." Question marks appear in blocks that were thought to need further study. For the most part these questionable blocks lie south and southeast of the main body of the CBD. Most of them have old factories specializing in some phase of jewelry manufacturing and with lots adjacent to the factories used for commercial parking. A pedestrian mall stretches along Westminster Street from Dorrance Street to Empire Street. Of course, a good deal of intensive field work would be necessary to bring out the CBD boundary in full and to determine land use and other CBD characteristics. This sort of preliminary reconnaissance by no means displaces the basic technique recommended. The full method as outlined in this chapter is sufficiently objective so that the areas delimited by workers in different cities should be comparable enough for generalizations about the CBD to carry some weight. The degree of detail of these generalizations, of course, will depend upon the detail of mapping.

The factor of comparability is important and should be kept in mind. For workers concerned entirely with their own city, such a method of delimitation as the one described ordinarily may serve little purpose. A boundary agreed upon locally may be adequate. But seldom does complete isolation prevail. The desire to compare the local CBD with that of some other city will arise, thus requiring the use of a standardized technique of delimitation. And when comparison of the CBDs of several cities is the major objective of a project, then a standardized method of outlining the CBDs is essential. It will be found desirable for such a comparison to use the detailed land-use classification earlier described since it yields much more data for comparison and generalization than the simple "C" and "X" classification.

Fig. 3.4. Central Providence, showing extent of CBD as determined by rapid field check

If it is desired to see how the CBD has changed in extent and character from a past period to the present within the same city, use of the CBI delimitation method may again be desirable. It is admittedly difficult to reconstruct a land-use map for an earlier period with sufficient accuracy so that the CBI method can be applied, but if an interval of only a decade or two is involved reasonably satisfactory results can probably be obtained.

The CBI method was developed in the 1950s and is sometimes objected to on the grounds that the work is out of date. Of course it is as far as the details of the boundaries of the nine CBDs are concerned and some of the generalizations, but the technique of delimitation still retains its value. The method remains the most practicable and realistic that has been advanced and the only one that gives reasonably comparable areas. And the generalizations already arrived at represent, we think, a substantial start on a tentative list.

4

Some Tentative Generalizations

The foregoing details regarding the CBI method of CBD delimitation are intended as a basis for outlining comparable areas, with the ultimate goal of arriving at generalizations. But the technique may also be used to advantage by any person or group wanting to delimit a CBD for their city. To that extent the method may serve a limited local and practical purpose.

To the originators of the method, however, much more important than any local value was the fact that each of the nine CBDs worked with—those of Grand Rapids, Mobile, Phoenix, Roanoke, Sacramento, Salt Lake City, Tacoma, Tulsa, and Worcester—was delimited on the same basis, and therefore they could be compared meaningfully. Instead of specific characteristics of uniquely identified areas, we would have a start toward tentative generalizations for CBDs of cities of the size group studied. These generalizations could be tested by additional studies in cities in the same size range, and the nine CBDs could also serve as norms with which similarly delimited CBDs of larger and of smaller cities might be compared.

Of course each city is unique in many respects. Hence, a variety of subjective factors are involved in any comparison. In the original work with the nine CBDs, such details were covered in a separate consideration of each of the nine urban centers. Among the topics considered for each were site, history, dominant city functions, land platting system, railroad influence, general setting of the CBD, general character and peculiarities of the CBD, tributary area, and extent of past PLVI movement.[1] Such background material is not subject to generalization, but it is essential to a real understanding of any individual CBD. However, going into such detail about each of the nine cities is outside the scope of this book. Here

---

1. See Raymond E. Murphy and J. E. Vance, Jr., "A Comparative Study of Nine Central Business Districts," *Economic Geography* 30 (1954): 301–336.

the concern is chiefly with describing and attempting to explain CBD size, shape, land valuation, and land use.

In this chapter some generalizations reached in the study of the nine CBDs are presented. They are not advanced as applicable to all CBDs, but rather as tentative generalizations based on the CBDs of nine moderate-sized urban centers which averaged a population of 151,000 in their incorporated cities in 1950 and an urbanized area population of 196,000 (for 1960 data see Appendix B).

Size of the CBD

The popular concept of CBD size is two-dimensional, and, of course, the district does occupy a certain gross area on the ground surface. That is one way of expressing size. On that basis, Worcester's CBD had an extent of 87.1 acres in the early 1950s and Tulsa's, 136.3 acres (see Appendix A).[2] Of the nine CBDs on which these generalizations are based, only two were larger than the Tulsa CBD: the Salt Lake City CBD, 189.4 acres and the Sacramento CBD, 188.2 acres. The average ground extent of the nine was 115.9 acres.

The foregoing is a simple approach to CBD size, but does it really tell the story? Obviously, the factor of height is neglected. The CBD is made up of upper floors as well as the ground floor, so volume should be a better measure to use in comparing CBD size than ground area. And since story heights are essentially standard, one might think of volume of a CBD as expressed by its total floor space at all levels. This can be obtained by adding the area of the second and higher floors to the area of the ground floor minus alleys. The advantage of total floor space as compared with simple ground-floor area is particularly evident in the case of Tulsa where the growth of office buildings has meant expansion of the CBD upward and hence a considerably greater percentage increase in total floor space than in CBD ground floor area. Indeed, a new 20-story office building in the CBD of any city need not be reflected at all in the ground-floor area of the district, but it would mean a definite increase in its total floor space.

Though total floor space in the CBD may be an improvement over gross ground-floor area in describing CBD size, it still leaves something to be desired. Too many land uses are included that do not belong in the district. Total central business space in the CBD is a better measure of CBD size since, in addition to taking height into consideration, it measures directly in central business units. Central business space in the CBD ranged from 75.5 acres for Mobile up to 207.7 acres for Tulsa in the nine-CBD study. The leading position of Tulsa reflects the city's population total and the growth of office buildings.

2. Such ground-area data can be obtained by planimeter measurements from a map on which the CBD has been delimited according to the method outlined in Chapter 3.

Determining what basis is to be used in defining CBDs is a necessary first step in a consideration of how CBDs vary in size from city to city and why. Unfortunately, the study of the nine CBDs on which the generalizations of this section are based did not yield much information about how CBDs vary with city size. To avoid too many variables, only cities within a limited range of sizes were included. But let us see what can be inferred from the CBDs that were studied.

It was naturally assumed in advance that CBD size would tend to increase with city size, and in a general way it does. Tulsa, with the most people, had more central business floor space in its CBD than any other of the nine cities. This relative relationship will be examined more closely to see what can be inferred from the nine cities.

It was assumed in advance of the nine-city study that CBD size, as measured by total central business floor space, might be found to vary directly with the population of the standard metropolitan statistical area, the urbanized area, or the corporate city. At least these possibilities were considered worth investigating. But little evidence was found of a relationship between CBD size and standard metropolitan statistical area population. More surprising was the fact that there was little evidence of CBD size varying with urbanized area population. Of the three types of areas mentioned, the urbanized area generally is regarded as most expressive of the contiguous urban area and hence most representative of the real city. There did appear to be a positive correlation between CBD size and incorporated city population.

The closer relationship of CBD size to corporate city population than to urbanized area population is difficult to explain. But a partial answer may lie in the fact that the urbanized area, at least in the range of city sizes used in the nine-city study, contained outlying built-up areas with their own stores outside the central city. These may have detracted from the importance and size of the central city's CBD. Such appears to be the case with Phoenix where several outlying surburban centers are large enough to compete seriously with the central city.

A rather close relationship, too, was found to exist between CBD size and such Census Bureau measures as retail employees in the incorporated city and wholesale employees in the incorporated city. In fact this relationship was so close that it seemed possible to use the number of employees in retailing or in wholesaling in the corporate city to estimate in advance the size of the CBD of a city. For example, each thousand retail trade employees appeared to mean some 12 or 13 acres of central business floor space. But it must be kept in mind that the cities studied did not vary significantly in size, and, therefore, any generalizations arrived at along these lines could be little more than preliminary suggestions.

If there are relationships such as those mentioned, they can well be expressed as ratios, for example, CBD size/incorporated city population,

CBD size/retail employees in incorporated city, and CBD size/wholesale employees in incorporated city. If the CBDs of much larger and much smaller cities were studied, would these ratios be found to remain about the same? Or would they vary with the size of the city? And just how? Would they vary with types of cities such as port cities, manufacturing cities, and state capitals? Use of the CBI method with several cities that ranged considerably in size should give us the answers to some of these questions.

Shape of the CBD

To most people the shape of the CBD is the outline that the district exhibits when depicted on a map. CBD shape was the basis for the work of George Hartman whose study was published in 1950.[3]

First, he considered the various theoretical possibilities of CBD shape (the circle, the star-like pattern, the diamond pattern), the bases for these patterns, and variations from the idealized arrangements. He emphasized the fact that in actuality each CBD has a spatial shape that in detail appears to be unique. But, in spite of the high degree of complexity and irregularity, definite geographic patterns are discernible. These patterns arise, Hartman said, from the fact that centralized commerical activities by their very nature operate under the same principle: they choose central positions with respect to all internal and external businesses in the city.

The multiplicity of actual shapes of central districts results from local conditions which are peculiar in detail to each district; it is these local conditions that produce variations from the idealized patterns. A geographic analysis of central business districts in various cities is best understood through a study of the various local factors which result in deviations from the theoretical spatial arrangement of the district.

Though he worked with "land use and related studies of approximately 40 cities in the United States," Hartman based his research on existing local maps rather than on his own mapping. CBD outlines thus obtained could hardly be expected to be very comparable. Nevertheless, his article is an interesting theoretical discussion of CBD plan-view shape.

The CBDs of the nine cities that form the chief basis for this chapter, when delimited according to the CBI method, showed a striking variety of outlines (Fig. 4.1). The detailed course of each boundary reflects block shapes since blocks are the units used in the delimitation. And there are many right angles as a result of the predominance of grid street patterns in so many American cities. Coarseness of outline was particularly noticeable in the CBD of Salt Lake City, a result of the fact that average block

3. George W. Hartman, "Central Business District, A Study in Urban Geography," *Economic Georgraphy* 26 (1950): 237–244.

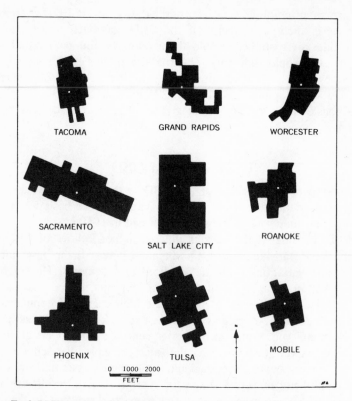

TACOMA   GRAND RAPIDS   WORCESTER

SACRAMENTO   ROANOKE

SALT LAKE CITY

PHOENIX   TULSA   MOBILE

0   1000   2000
FEET

Note: Each PLVI appears as a white dot.
Source: Raymond E. Murphy and J. E. Vance, Jr., "A Comparative Study of Nine Central Business Districts," *Economic Geography* 30 (1954), Fig. 22.

Fig. 4.1. Plan views of the nine CBDs as delimited using the CBI method

size there is more than three times that of any of the other eight districts. Had the delimitation technique been based on lots instead of blocks the various CBDs would have shown much the same irregularity of outline but finer edge detail. (See, for example, Fig. 2.2.)

Looking broadly at the CBD outlines of the nine cities, one sees little evidence of the star-like pattern or of the "tilted square or diamond" pattern that were postulated as possibilities by Hartman. The former is hardly to be expected since none of the nine CBDs studied in detail had radial streets sufficient in number to result in such an outline. But since grid patterns predominate, and since in many instances the CBD has two principal, intersecting (and hence radial) streets, a tilted square or diamond might be expected.

However, it seems unrealistic to think of the space between the radial streets as having been filled in sufficiently to form a true diamond, since location on or near one or another of the radial streets is so important for central business functions. Filling in of the CBD between the radials goes on near the PLVI, but with increasing distance from the center these "in between" areas rapidly lose their attractiveness for central business activities. Instead of a diamond, therefore, the idealized outline is more nearly a four-pointed figure with concave sides, or, more accurately, a quadrate cross (Fig. 4.2). There is a suggestion of this shape in the CBD of Phoenix

Source: Raymond E. Murphy and J. E. Vance, Jr., "A Comparative Study of Nine Central Business Districts," *Economic Geography* 30 (1954), Fig. 24.

Fig. 4.2. The idealized outline of the CBD is best approximated by a quadrate cross

(Fig. 4.1), and, although it is not much in evidence in the shape of the Worcester CBD as outlined on a block basis according to the CBI method (Fig. 3.2), it is clearly to be seen on the map of the district delimited on a lot basis by land values (Fig. 2.2). It is probable, too, that the current ribbon development along streets leading away from the PLVIs of various cities is causing many districts to approximate more and more the quadrate cross outline. Clearly, larger cities, especially if they have a number of radial streets, are less likely to show the quadrate cross form.

The concept of an idealized outline, whether quadrate cross or diamond, is based on the idea of two intersecting thoroughfares of equal importance. Actually, this perfect balance is probably never found, so no district can be expected to achieve more than a rough resemblance to the theoretical shape. When the two intersecting thoroughfares differ considerably in importance, the district becomes elongated along one axis. Relative equality of several parallel axes tends to produce a broad, elongated CBD.

The shapes presented by the CBDs of the nine cities might be classified as follows (Fig. 4.1): (1) fairly equivalent intersecting axes, an approximation of a quadrate cross—Phoenix, Roanoke, Mobile, and, to a certain degree, Worcester; (2) dominant single street with resulting elongation of the CBD—Worcester, Grand Rapids, Sacramento; (3) parallel streets that exceed in importance any crossing street, with a resulting block-like CBD—Tulsa, Salt Lake City, and possibly Tacoma.

But the CBD, as was pointed out, is not just two-dimensional. It might well be thought of as some modification of a pyramid. If we follow the idea that the CBD outline is diamond-shaped, then the pyramid would have a square base, and each of the four corners would rest on one of the four radiating streets. If, however, we think of the quadrate cross in place of a diamond, the solid would no longer be a simple pyramid; it would have to be visualized as a pyramid with concave slopes.

The base corresponds to the ground-floor area of the CBD. The volume amounts to the central business floor space in the CBD, which, as was pointed out earlier, may be thought of as volume since a uniform story-height is assumed.

The height may be calculated by using the formula $V = 1/3\ Bh$. Applying this formula to each of the nine CBDs (Appendix A) the following pyramid heights were obtained: Tulsa, 7.8 stories; Grand Rapids, 7.2 stories; Worcester, 6.0 stories; Roanoke, 5.8 stories; Tacoma, 5.7 stories; Salt Lake City, 4.6 stories; Sacramento, 4.6 stories; Mobile, 4.5 stories; and Phoenix 4.4 stories.

This concept is theoretical, but it has some value in contrasting CBDs. Certainly, Tulsa, with its concentrated office growth, stands out in contrast to Phoenix. Do the newer, Southwestern cities tend, in general, to have lower, flatter CBDs than cities in other sections of the country? Do the CBDs of Southern cities differ from those of other parts of the country in certain characteristic aspects? Is a typical American city CBD in the process of evolution?

CBD Shape in Relation to Barriers

To what extent is the shape of a typical CBD related to barriers that surround or interrupt it? (Fig. 4.3.) That there are barriers to the expansion of the CBD is obvious. Otherwise, idealized and symmetrical patterns would be more common. Railroads, arterial streets, water bodies, parks, areas devoted to public buildings, and a variety of other tangible land uses have molded the CBD's shape and extent through permitting or favoring local growth in one direction or another. In some cases, the CBD may approach the barrier closely. This usually happens with public buildings, where the CBD may be adjacent to them or occasionally surround them.

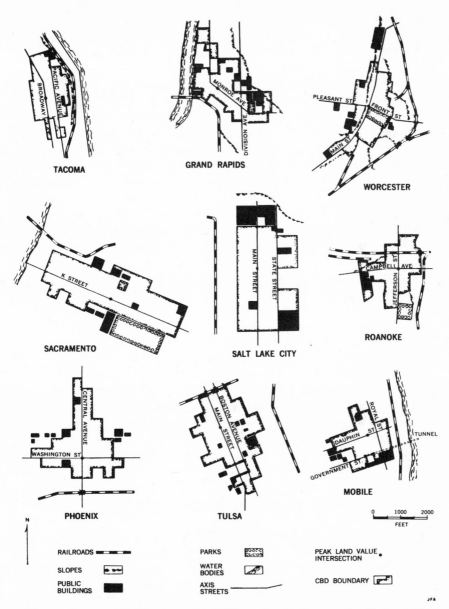

Source: Raymond E. Murphy and J. E. Vance, Jr., "A Comparative Study of Nine Central Business Districts," *Economic Geography* 30 (1954), Fig. 23.

Fig. 4.3. Barriers affect the outline of a CBD by limiting expansion in certain directions

It happens also in the case of parks. But where there are railroad and water bodies, the CBD does not, usually, abut directly upon them. There is commonly a cushion of other uses between the CBD and the barrier.

Relief as a barrier deserves special mention. There is no doubt but that steep slopes serve as an obstacle to accessibility and hence to CBD development. If it is at all possible such slopes are avoided, but there are examples of their being used, just as there are occasional cases of a CBD extending across a railroad or continuing on the far side of a freeway.

Just how important these tangible barriers are in helping to determine the shape of a CBD is difficult to assess. Thus Grand Rapids and Worcester, both with tall, compact CBDs, are hampered by barriers. But Tulsa's CBD, which is even taller and even more compact, is not particularly restricted by tangible barriers. Obviously, there are other barriers to expansion of a CBD than tangible, physical ones. There are, for example, such legal barriers as those set by zoning ordinances and laws restricting certain heights and types of buildings in an area.

It has been suggested that CBDs tend also to be limited by a distance factor. The district has been called a "walking zone." Since people usually walk from one part of the CBD to another, there is a certain amount of reluctance to use areas that are located too far from the PLVI for easy walking. In American cities of the size here considered, however, the distance factor is offset by the fact that in marginal sections of a CBD, where more space is available for parking, the automobile can be used. There seems to be a marginal zone in a normal CBD that might be called the "automobile-oriented zone." Perhaps the walking zone is coincident with the so-called hard core of the CBD, and the automobile-oriented zone is related to the part of the CBD that lies just outside the hard core.

However, sooner or later, the CBD comes to an edge where other uses take over and the number of floors of central business use plus the intensity of each use does not warrant including a block in the CBD. This border will be reached in CBDs that are uninhibited by barriers as well as in those that are more restricted. But no doubt the breaking point comes sooner in a direction in which a CBD has to overcome tangible barriers than it does in other directions.

Although we have been talking about the effects of barriers on the CBD outline, we know that the CBD has a height factor as well as horizontal dimensions. How is this three-dimensional shape affected by barriers? The effect is often not as obvious nor as indisputable as in the case of CBD outline. Chiefly, it is a matter of barriers affecting the normal spread of a CBD, resulting in an abnormal expansion upward. Manhattan, hemmed in by water, is perhaps the prime example of this, but many cities show the effect to some degree. However, it may be difficult in any specific case to determine exactly how much barrier-imposed space limitations have been responsible for the vertical expansion. Other factors such as site prestige, local pride in tall buildings, and even whims of individuals or concerns must be considered.

Land Values and CBD Structure

The nine-CBD study also yielded some information on typical land-value variations associated with the CBD. Of course, land value is based on man's estimate of the potential of a piece of land rather than on the use to which it is being put. The land-values map of a city is likely to show the highest values around the main business intersection, a fact that holds true whether the land is empty or is occupied by department stores.

Since property values are commonly recorded by lots, the lot was the land unit used in our work on land values. It was pointed out in an earlier chapter of this book that, for the group of CBDs studied, a line could be drawn for each CBD enclosing all lots whose front-foot land values equaled 5 per cent or more of that of the highest-valued lot, and that this 5 per cent line roughly approximated the CBD edge as determined by the CBI method. Figure 4.4 shows six of the cities for which land-value data were obtained in the nine-city study. Land value data were not available for three of the nine CBDs, so remarks made here are based on only six cities: Grand Rapids, Phoenix, Sacramento, Salt Lake City, Tacoma, and Worcester.

Broadly, land values in each of the six CBDs were found to range from the peak value down to about 5 per cent of that amount at the district's edge. Other percentage lines were drawn on the same basis as the 5 per cent line, but they are not shown in Figure 4.4. In these cities the 5 per cent line, though not coinciding exactly with the CBD boundaries based on land use, generally did not depart very far from them. But some differences are to be expected. In part this results from lots forming the basis for the land-value lines and blocks for the CBDs based on land use, and there is the added fact that land values do not discriminate among land uses. The drawing of the 5 per cent line (enclosing the area of the city with front-foot values amounting to 5 per cent or more of those of the peak value lot) and the other lines for higher percentages presented numerous problems. Because of these difficulties no attempt has been made to show on the maps the full series of land-value lines. In places, successive land-value lines coincided; in others, lots intervened that were public land or other untaxable property that had no valuation. Hence, subjective judgments frequently were involved.

Nevertheless, in each case, eleven land-value classes were determined: one extremely small one consisting of the lot or lots having peak valuation (100 per cent), one made up of lots amounting to at least 5 but less than

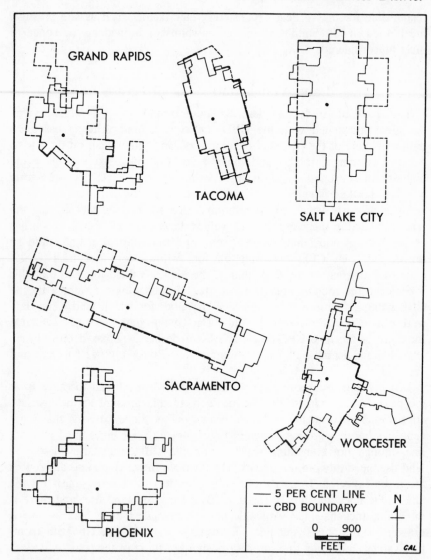

Note: The dot represents, in each case, a PLVI.
Source: Raymond E. Murphy, J. E. Vance, Jr., and Bart J. Epstein, "Internal Structure of the CBD," *Economic Geography* 31 (1955), Fig. 1.

Fig. 4.4. The 5 per cent land value lines and their CBD boundaries in six CBDs

10 per cent of the peak value, and the remaining nine dividing the values between 10 and 100. For each of these eleven classes the total acreage in the six cities was measured and combined.

Some interesting facts became apparent. Perhaps the most striking was that three-fourths of the area within the 5 per cent line was found to be valued at less than 20 per cent of the peak value lot. Only a little more than 8 per cent was valued at as much as half the peak value. In other words, land values were found to decrease rapidly at first with distance from the PLVI, but this decline becomes less and less rapid toward the edges of the district. The average curve of decline is somewhat irregular but clearly concave. The situation can be summed up by saying that land values decrease at a decreasing rate with distance from the PLVI.

Of course, these facts are based on an average of the six districts, and they assume a symmetrically shaped CBD. This symmetry is rarely found, but there is a tendency for successive percentage lines roughly to parallel the outline of each district. In other words, from the PLVI, values on the average decline outward, though higher-than-average values continue from the center along the main thoroughfares, and the rate of decline is much lower along the axis of the district than at right angles to it. Since so much of the discussion on land values in the CBD depends upon the location of the PLVI, calculations were made to determine the relative locations of this critical point and the geographic center of each of the nine districts (Fig. 4.5). In the nine cities the PLVI was nowhere found to be more than a few hundred feet from the geographic or areal center of the CBD. Naturally, in most cases, the geographic center lies in the direction from the PLVI in which maximum growth of the CBD has been occurring. (Compare with Figure 4.10.)

Land-Use Generalizations

In the original study of the nine CBD's, the development of a delimitation technqiue was only one of the objectives; in fact, it was regarded largely as a way station on the road. The particular interest was in arriving at generalizations, especially land-use generalizations, since these were considered to promise more than those dealing with size, shape, and land values. A further objective was to gain more information regarding the exact land-use variations in CBDs than a simple classification into central business uses and non-central business uses permitted.

Figure 4.6 shows floor-space devoted to various uses for each of the nine CBD's and for an average of all of them. The bars are proportional in width to total floor space in the CBDs. The proportions shown are based on field mapping carried on during 1952 and 1953. It is important to keep in mind that the picture presented by each bar in the chart is one of land use in the CBD, not in the city. For example, a smaller proportion of automotive sales is shown for Worcester than for most of the other eight cities. This does not mean that, in Worcester, automotive sales are less important than in the other cities. It merely means that less of this business is carried on within the Worcester CBD than in most of the other CBDs. Automotive sales in Worcester happen to be concentrated in several areas that

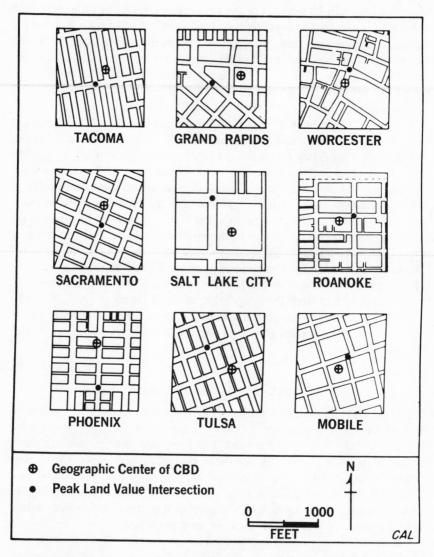

Source: Raymond E. Murphy, J. E. Vance, Jr., and Bart J. Epstein, "Internal Structure of the CBD," *Economic Geography* 31 (1955), Fig. 2.

Fig. 4.5. PLVIs and geographic centers for the nine CBDs

are well outside the CBD. (For numerical data on floor-space proportions see Appendix C.)

Some of the information resulting is to be expected. For example, by definition of the CBD, central business uses (retail business and service-financial-office uses) predominate over non-central business uses, and certain

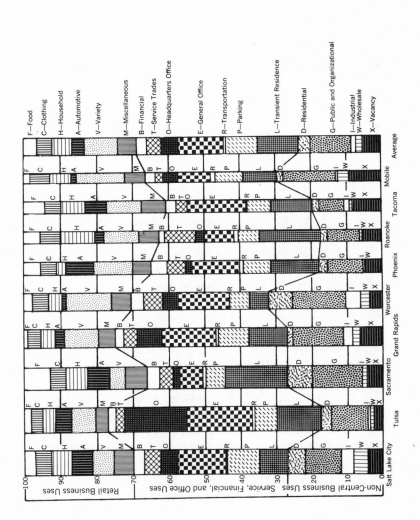

Fig. 4.6. Floor-space proportions devoted to various uses for each of the nine CBDs and for an average of all of them

Source: Raymond E. Murphy and J. E. Vance, Jr., "A Comparative Study of Nine Central Business Districts," *Economic Geography* 30 (1954), Fig. 25

land uses, such as manufacturing, wholesaling (with stocks), and permanent residences, are largely eliminated so their low proportions in CBDs are not surprising. In addition, a detailed classification is used which makes it possible to determine differences in the exact land uses of the several CBDs (Appendix C).

Though in the original study the land-use picture of each CBD was described and explained, such details are beyond the scope of this book. But the average of the nine CBDs is probably the most important of the land-use generalizations resulting from the study. As additional CBDs are delimited, it is interesting to compare their averages with the average of the nine districts. Similar data for the CBDs of the larger cities delimited according to the CBI method would add significantly to our picture of the CBD. They would give more of a basis for generalizations about variations in CBD land uses with city size and character and would make it possible to say with some assurance what land-use proportions would be likely to characterize the CBD of a city of any given size.

Arrangement of Land Uses

Other results of the study of the nine CBDs included generalizations regarding the arrangement of business activities within the district in the average moderate-sized American city. As a basis for studying the arrangement of land uses, a pattern of four walking-distance zones was constructed on acetate paper for each CBD.[4] Zone 1 was the area surrounding the PLVI to a distance of 100 yards measured along streets. The points thus determined were linked by diagonal lines drawn across blocks to form a continuous line. Three concentric zones (Zones 2, 3, and 4) were drawn around this core area. The outer boundaries measured along streets from the PLVI were 200, 300, and 400 yards respectively. Obviously, Zone 1 is a solid, compact area surrounding the PLVI, and the other zones are merely belts of land surrounding Zone 1.

The pattern of zones on acetate paper for each CBD was used as an overlay on the land-use maps, thus making it possible to tabulate the use data by distance zones and, at the same time, to calculate areas of use units. In the analysis, each establishment was considered to lie completely in the zone in which it fronted; in questionable cases preference was given to the lower-numbered zones. It should be noted that the analysis applies only to the area within 400-yards walking distance of the PLVI and only to that part of the area so described that is within the CBD.

Eight of the nine CBDs were included in the land-use analysis since the mapping in Roanoke was done too late for that CBD to be included. The

---

4. See Raymond E. Murphy, J. E. Vance, Jr., and Bart J. Epstein, "Internal Structure of the CBD," *Economic Geography* 31 (1955): 24–40.

information resulting from the map analysis of the eight CBDs was presented graphically on a percentage basis. One chart represented an average of the eight (Fig. 4.7), but there were separate graphs for each of the eight CBDs for which data were available. The Sacramento chart is included here as an example (Fig. 4.8). In every instance the land uses represented in the columns are divided into three groups—Retail Business; Service, Financial, and Office; and Non-Central Business—and these groups in turn are broken down into more detailed use types.

It is of interest to look more closely at the changes in land use with increasing distance outward through the CBD (Table 4.1). In the inner zone, around the PLVI, there are likely to be one or more variety or department stores (with such closely related establishments as clothing stores, Fig. 4.9) one or two banks, drugstores, five-and-ten-cent stores, restaurants, and miscellaneous specialty stores. In a few cities, a city hall and a park or

Table 4.1   Relative rank-order of the four zones in proportion of space occupied by various types of establishments in the eight CBDs

	Zones			
	1	*2*	*3*	*4*
RETAIL BUSINESS USES	1	2	3	4
Food	4	3	1	2
Clothing	1	2	3	4
Household	4	3	2	1
Automotive	n.r.	3	2	1
Variety	1	2	3	4
Miscellaneous	4	1	3	2
SERVICE-FINANCIAL-OFFICE USES	4	1	2	3
Financial	4	2	1	3
Headquarters Office	3[a]	2[a]	1	4
General Office	3	1	2	4
Service Trades	4	2	3	1
Transportation	4[a]	3[a]	2[a]	1[a]
Transient residence	4	2[a]	3	1[a]
Parking	4	2[a]	3[a]	1
NON-CENTRAL BUSINESS USES	4	3	2	1
Public and organizational	4	3	1[a]	2[a]
Residential	n.r.	3[a]	2[a]	1
Wholesale	n.r.	3	2	1
Industrial	n.r.	1	3	2
Vacancy	1	4	3	2

n.r. Not represented in zone.

[a]Approximately equal to others with similar superscripts in the same horizontal line.

Note: Compare with Sec. I, Fig. 4.7.

Source: Murphy and Vance, "Delimiting the CBD," *Economic Geography* 30 (1954).

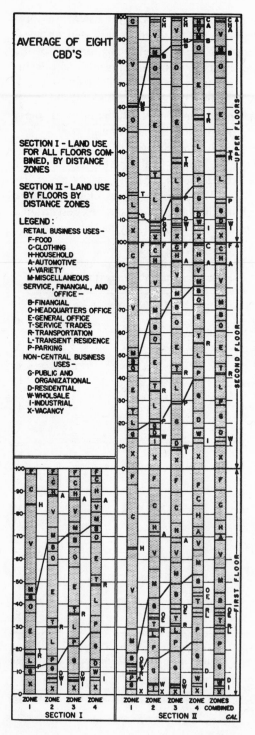

Source: Raymond E. Murphy, J. E. Vance, Jr., and Bart Epstein, "Internal Structure of the CBD," *Economic Geography* 31 (1955), Fig. 3.

Fig. 4.7. Land-use analysis by distance zones for an average of the eight CBDs

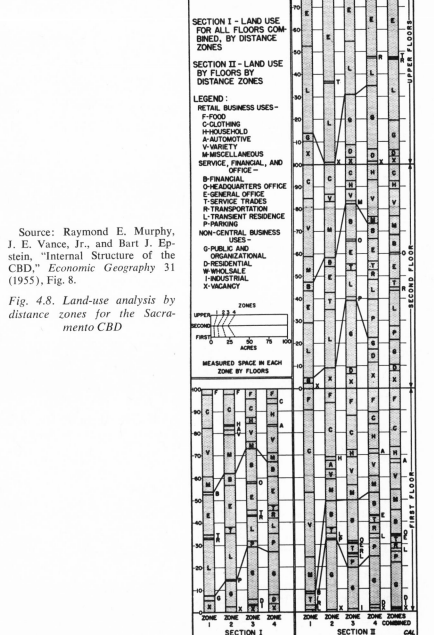

Source: Raymond E. Murphy, J. E. Vance, Jr., and Bart J. Epstein, "Internal Structure of the CBD," *Economic Geography* 31 (1955), Fig. 8.

Fig. 4.8. Land-use analysis by distance zones for the Sacramento CBD

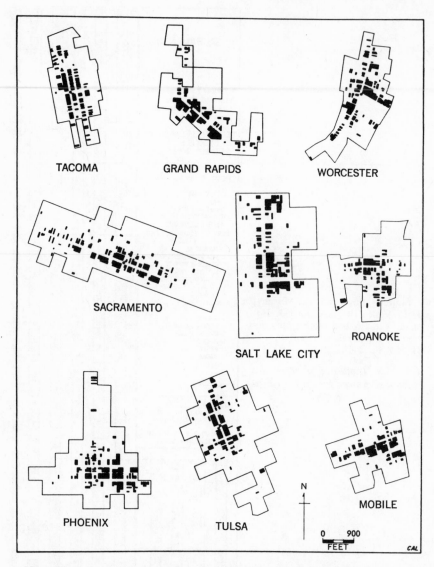

Note: These two types of stores, shown in black on the map, are alike in extending closer to the PLVI, the small circle appearing in each CBD, than most other types of establishments. Based on ground-floor use only.

Source: Raymond E. Murphy, J. E. Vance, Jr., and Bart J. Epstein, "Internal Structure of the CBD," *Economic Geography* 31 (1955), Fig. 12.

Fig. 4.9. Variety stores and clothing stores in the nine CBDs

common may occur near the PLVI. One thing is true of most stores in the inner zone: for their kind, they are likely to be large. Here one finds the CBD's largest department stores, the largest drugstores, the largest five-and-ten-cent stores.

It is somewhat of a paradox that the centermost point of the city does not commonly have the tallest buildings (Table 4.2). Although substantial buildings often occur around the PLVI, even taller buildings are likely to be found a little farther from this point, with retail services and financial activities occupying the ground floor, and offices dominating the floors above. Some of the city's tallest buildings have been built to house the

Table 4.2 Location by zones of the higher buildings in the CBD

	Ratio of Total Floor Space at Sixth Floor Level and Higher to Ground Floor Area of the Zone			
	Zone 1	*Zone 2*	*Zone 3*	*Zone 4*
Worcester	.03	.67	.26	.26
Grand Rapids	.17	.70	1.41	.49
Salt Lake City	.67	.25	.06	.16
Tacoma	.11	.33	.33	.57
Sacramento	.39	.13	.16	.12
Phoenix	.00	.16	.42	.22
Tulsa	1.02	2.08	1.16	.85
Mobile	.00	.37	.28	.00
Average for eight cities	.30	.59	.51	.33

Source: Murphy and Vance, "Delimiting the CBD," *Economic Geography* 30 (1954).

central or regional offices of single companies. More often, however, office buildings contain a number of individual units, and frequently these units do a considerable amount of business with one another. Banks often occupy corners at the PLVI, but they are more commonly situated in the belt 200–300 yards from the peak point. Hotels, too, are most important at about this distance from the center.

Near the edge of the district such establishments as furniture stores and automotive stores are typical, and, still farther out, often spilling over the edge, one finds automobile sales rooms (with associated garages and filling stations) and supermarkets, both land uses that require reasonably cheap land but much parking space as well. This area, close to the boundary of the CBD, is often automobile-oriented, especially where it occurs near the end of an elongated district.

The CBD has a vertical dimension, especially near its center. With distance upward from the ground floor, through successive stories, retailing and certain of the service and financial uses decline in space occupied, and offices increase (Fig. 4.7). A few words about office space are in order. In the nine-city study it was found that the chief demand for office space was in new, high office buildings. Office vacancies were greatest in old cities, in cities that had grown old before their time, and above all in old buildings.

Land-Use Associations

Distance from the PLVI is not the only motivating factor that helps to determine where a given type of land use will be found in the CBD. If it were, the typical CBD would consist of a series of concentric zones, each with unique uses. And this pattern, obviously, does not prevail. There is, among other things, a noticeable clustering of establishments mutually dependent upon one another. To some extent, of course, every enterprise in the CBD depends upon all of the others, for the whole assemblage generates the mass of customers upon which the district depends.

The relationship between certain kinds of establishments, however, is often much more compelling than mere dependence upon the whole assemblage. There is, for example, the well-known tendency of department stores to locate near each other. And there are recognized associations of stores which seem to occur repeatedly. Each department store, for instance, is likely to have its coterie of smaller stores such as clothing stores, drugstores, five-and-ten-cent stores, located close at hand. Not only do these stores seek the same type of location, near the heart of the CBD where the pedestrian count is high, but they all profit by being available to the customers attracted by the others and particularly by the large department store, which is the dominant member of the group.

Other groupings can readily be picked out. Stores handling office supplies and furniture usually have associated themselves with office buildings. Lawyers' offices, real estate offices, and bail bond agencies often form a group near the court house. Low-prices theaters are likely to be associated with kindred low-priced establishments such as pawn shops, cheap restaurants, and stores handling low-priced jewelry or clothing. Men's clothing stores of the better class may make either of two types of affiliations. They may be found near the large department stores where they are readily available to women shoppers who buy for the family; or they may be located near banks and office buildings where they depend largely on the men who work in these places.

Clustering, of course, is not confined to the ground floor level. There is vertical clustering as well. This is particularly apparent in office buildings, where various kinds of offices seem to benefit from close association with one another. Lawyers, insurance brokers, and real estate agents frequently locate together. Physicians often profit from close association to the extent that whole sections of buildings or complete small office buildings may be devoted to their offices. The ultimate along this line is reached in the headquarters office building, where all but the ground floor and sometimes even that, may be devoted to the business offices of a single firm.

These points constitute only a brief summary of some of the ideas of land-use associations characterizing CBDs,[5] but some of the more obvious

5. For a fuller treatment of land-use associations for the city as a whole see Richard U. Ratcliff, *The Problem of Retail Site Selection,* Michigan Business Studies,

clustering tendencies have been noted. An appreciation of these associations is vital to an understanding of CBD structure.

There is the further complicating factor that the associative tendencies themselves are constantly changing. Food stores, for example, which used to be a typical land use associated with department stores and other stores patronized by women shoppers, have been moving from the CBD, leaving only a few food specialty shops (bakeries, delicatessens, candy stores) as remnants of a once-important land-use type. A similar trend can be detected in some types of variety stores. In general, those types of retailing that depend upon frequent, day-to-day shopping seem prone to move out of the CBD, leaving at the city's center only those stores that depend upon infrequent or highly specialized sales.

Dynamic Aspects of CBD Structure

It need hardly be pointed out that the CBD is not static. It is highly mobile in spite of the great investment in land and buildings it represents. The picture of the CBD, however sharp and accurate it may seem, is no more than a glimpse of the moment. It reflects the past in the original site conditions and in changes through time, the present in its response to current economic conditions; and it carries a forecast of the future.

The minutiae of changes going on in the average CBD are almost impossible to unravel, but there are broad elements that can be described which help to rationalize the picture. For instance, it is a simple matter to recognize that the margins of the district are constantly fluctuating, advancing here and retreating there. Specific transportation features—port works, railroad stations, early road junctions—generally were responsible for the original location of the city. This initial development, in turn, formed the nucleus of the modern CBD. As the city grew, the CBD may have become more and more off-center for the urban area as a whole and the pressure for some shift in the position of the district correspondingly great, as seen particularly in port cities. It is a matter of record that the PLVI of many CBDs has shifted from time to time in the past. Let us look at these dynamic elements a little more thoroughly.

It has been assumed that a CBD tends to expand if the city is growing and to contract if the the city is not growing. But the nine CBDs on which this chapter is largely based failed to confirm this assumption. All the CBDs studied showed evidences of advancing along certain fronts and retreating along others. Thus, there are zones of assimilation and zones of discard (Fig. 4.10). What is the nature of these areas and where are they likely to occur?

Several authors have pointed out that the district tends to move toward

vol. 9, no. 1 (Ann Arbor: Bureau of Business Research, University of Michigan, 1939) and *Urban Land Economics* (New York: McGraw-Hill Book Co., Inc., 1949).

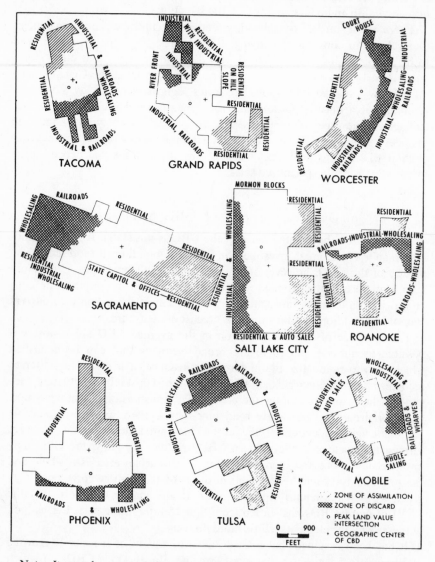

Note: It may be assumed that the white areas are essentially static or balanced.
Source: Raymond E. Murphy, J. E. Vance, Jr., and Bart J. Epstein, "Internal Structure of the CBD," *Economic Geography* 31 (1955), Fig. 16.

Fig. 4.10. Approximate positions of Zone of Assimilation and Zone of Discard in each of the nine CBDs

areas of higher residential quality. This process was observable in the nine cities, but the reasons for the movement seem to be negative. It may be due not so much to the high-class residential area's attracting the CBD as to the fact that the industrial-wholesaling district near the railroads, with its attendant low-class housing, tends to repel the CBD. If movement takes place, it must occur at the expense of the better residential areas, areas that have, in fact, already begun to feel the competition for space from the more aggressive businesses in the adjacent CBD.

It follows that the CBD will show differing land-use characteristics in its zone of assimilation and its zone of discard. In the zone of assimilation, specialty shops, automobile show rooms, drive-in banks, headquarters offices, professional offices, and the newer hotels are likely to be found. In the rear, on the other hand, in the zone of discard, one finds pawn shops, family clothing stores, bars, low-grade restaurants, bus stations, cheap movies, and credit jewelry, clothing, and furniture stores. These low-grade establishments depend in part upon the tendency toward clustering mentioned earlier since they appeal to the same economic level. The zone of discard has furnished sites for wholesaling (with stocks), too, but nowadays such wholesaling seems to be drawn more to industrial parks entirely outside the CBD.[6] In the whole picture the factor of prestige enters. The zone of assimilation is the land of the future, whereas the zone of discard lacks prestige and fosters commercial types that make no pretense of being more than places to sell goods and services.

The size and shape of the CBD are constantly changing. As the CBD shifts, the PLVI is likely to move also. This change is to be expected. In the nine CBDs studied, the PLVI was found to be close to the geographic center of the CBD, only a few hundred feet away in most cases (Fig. 4.5). If the whole area changes its position, the geographic center will move and so eventually will the PLVI.

Let us look more closely at the manner in which the PLVI moves and the underlying causes for its movement. At this critical intersection, where the land values are high and where there is a tremendous focusing of travel, large investments in the form of buildings are likely to be made. When the district shifts its balance, causing a focus of travel elsewhere, there is at first a great reluctance to abandon the investments around the original PLVI. The pull toward a newer site must build up slowly. Eventually, when the demand is great enough, buildings will be constructed at a new intersection and their presence will help to make that location more attractive.

The movement of the PLVI, then, is not one of steady progress from one point to another, but rather one of leapfrogging, one or two blocks at a time. Few cities can boast that their present CBD's central zone, around the PLVI, is the same as the original center. Derelict centers are particularly characteristic of cities that began near a water front or a railroad station. This whole subject of the movement of CBD centers and of the way the district itself shifts is an important one for further study.

6. See J. E. Vance, Jr., *The Merchant's World: the Geography of Wholesaling* (Englewood Cliffs, N.J., Prentice-Hall, Inc., 1970), p. 26.

Further Studies and Further Generalizations Needed

The tentative generalizations presented in this chapter are by no means a summary of all findings from the nine-city study. However, the most important ones have been discussed, and they should suffice to illustrate the possibilities of such research.

More studies of CBDs are needed. The districts of larger cities, especially, need to be mapped and analyzed, so that the relationships between CBD size and city size can be worked out more fully. It would be of interest to study the CBDs of various types of cities—port cities, manufacturing centers, state capitals, etc.—to see what diagnostic characteristics each has. Intriguing, too, is the question of how CBDs differ regionally. Is there a typical Western or Southwestern CBD? Do the CBDs of Southern cities differ from those in other parts of the country? Is a typical CBD of the American city in the process of evolution?

Certainly, one characteristic that needs studying is CBD quality. In the delimitation technique used in the nine-city study no measure of quality was included, yet the researchers were well aware of definite contrasts between CBDs in this regard. It is undoubtedly true, for instance, that the CBD of Tulsa is of much higher average quality than that of Tacoma. But quality is complex. It includes more than the value of buildings and the level of merchandise handled by the stores. There is a dynamic aspect, too. It involves the questions of whether, through the erection of new buildings and the remodeling of old ones, a city's CBD is being kept up-to-date, and whether the district really reflects the potential of the area it serves. Subjective judgments are not sufficient to bring out such contrasts, but a good objective measure of CBD quality remains to be developed.

There are a number of specific topics that might be investigated within the framework of the CBD. There seems to have been no adequate treatment of CBD manufacturing. The subject of vacancy within CBDs is another interesting topic as is the active commercialization of basements which characterizes some CBDs. The idea of zones of assimilation and of discard needs to be followed up. And there are various other possibilities.

Further Generalizations

This summary of tentative generalizations has been based on the nine-CBD research project that was the starting point for this book. But it represents only a beginning. Many people have been contributing directly or indirectly to our knowledge of the downtown, and in the chapters that follow various investigations will be summarized. Some are based on CBI-delimited districts; many are not. But they all give insights into the CBD and its problems and thus broaden our knowledge of this unique region.

5

Cape Town's CBD

In the years that followed the appearance of the several papers resulting from the nine-CBD research project, little was done in the United States with the CBI delimitation technique or with CBDs delimited on this basis. Apparently, the method was used successfully by some planners in moderate-sized cities, and it is rumored that it was used with modifications in larger cities. But these were practical applications in planning and nothing appeared in the literature relevant to the work.

The method was tried abroad, however, in several cities and the results published. They will be summarized in this and the following chapter with particular emphasis upon problems of technique that arose and upon what the studies add to CBD philosophy and methodology. The two papers abstracted in this chapter focused upon Cape Town and are the work of D. Hywel Davies.

A General Study of the CBD of Cape Town

The most rigorous application and testing of the CBI method for delimiting the CBD that followed the original work is represented by D. Hywel Davies' general study of Cape Town's CBD.[1] Although he was concerned with delimitation methods, Davies also showed how this sort of investigation could lead to a deeper understanding of the CBD's character and problems. His paper is a long one; only the major features are presented here.

Davies began with a discussion of the site and urban setting of Cape Town's CBD (Fig. 5.1). The district occupies the flattest land at the center of the amphitheater formed by Table Mountain and its northeastern and

1. D. Hywel Davies, "Boundary Study as a Tool in CBD Analysis: An Interpretation of Certain Aspects of the Boundary of Cape Town's Central Business District," *Economic Geography* 35 (1959): 322–345.

northwestern extensions. Davies described the expansion of the city in this
setting: how Cape Town proper filled the amphitheater and the spectacular growth of the outer suburbs that ensued. At the time he wrote, the
urban agglomeration had attained a population of some 700,000. Thus, it

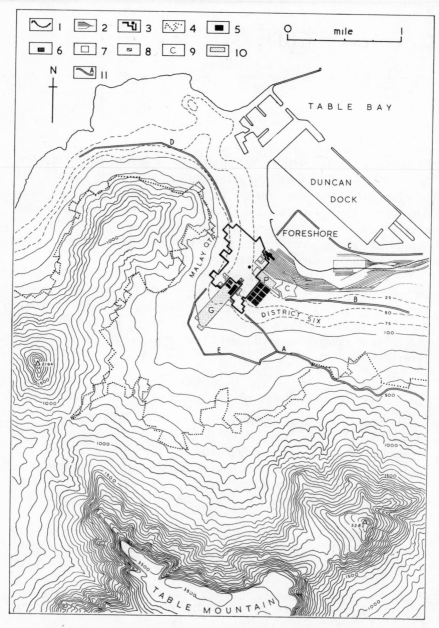

Fig. 5.1. Site of Cape Town's CBD

was a great deal larger than any of the nine American cities on whose CBDs the generalizations of Chapter 4 are based. As in most port cities, the CBD has now been left very much off-center by the growth of the total urban area and is in the oldest and most restricted part of *greater* Cape Town. Despite physical restrictions on the growth of Cape Town, the CBD has a natural tendency to exert pressure on the immediately surrounding residential areas. In the face of this pressure, some of the inner residential sections are deteriorating into areas of "urban blight," overcrowded slums interspersed with warehouses, wholesale establishments, and small industries.

Three barriers have interfered with CBD expansion, each operating on a particular section of the boundary. The first is the physical barrier imposed progressively by relief as the mountain slopes are approached. But the CBD occupies a relatively small, central area of a wide amphitheater, and relief has affected its growth only toward the northwest. The second barrier was imposed by the shoreline of Table Bay and the railway line to the Docks which ran along it. Reclamation of the Foreshore between 1938 and 1945, however, provided another 160 acres for CBD development. The term "Foreshore" is applied to a large area of reclaimed land between the new Duncan Dock and the old shoreline at the northeast corner of the CBD.

The third barrier is man-made and is present on the southeastern and southwestern sides where there are no physical barriers. It consists of provincial, national, and municipal administrative buildings that reflect Cape Town's important role as a government center. These administrative blocks are essentially non-CBD in character and in effect oppose the expansion of the CBD. And there are other individual blocks with various types of public functions which locally stand in the way of CBD expansion. Until the relatively recent reclamation of the Foreshore, therefore, the CBD with minor exceptions was restricted on all sides, thus increasing the tendency for upward growth.

Davies encountered no special difficulties in applying the CBI technique

---

Key to legend: 1. The 1938 shoreline; 2. Railway yards; 3. CBD boundary; 4. Inner (mountain-slope) margins of built-up area; 5. Government and municipal blocks lying immediately beyond the CBD boundary; 6. St. George's Cathedral and School; 7. Government and municipal blocks within the CBD; 8. Groote Kerk; 9. Castle; 10. Public open spaces lying immediately beyond CBD boundary; 11. Major roads A: Roeland St.–de Waal; B: Darling St.–Sir Lowry Rd.; C: National Road; D: Somerset Rd.–Main Rd.; E: Long St.–Orange St. Contours are drawn at 100-foot intervals; in addition, the 25', 50', and 75' contours are shown by means of broken lines. The passenger sections of the railway termini are shown within the CBD, other sections outside its boundary. The smaller Dock Area northwest of the Duncan Dock is the Victoria Basin. The promontory lying WNW of the Malay Quarter is Signal Hill.

Source: D. Hywel Davies, "Boundary Study as a Tool in CBD Analysis: An Interpretation of Certain Aspects of the Boundary of Cape Town's Central Business District," *Economic Geography* 35 (1959), Fig. 2.

to central Cape Town, though three minor modifications were found necessary.

The first was that instead of constructing just three maps—ground-floor, second-floor, and upper-floors—four were made: ground-floor, second-floor, third-floor, and a composite of upper-floors. This modification was considered desirable because the substantial size of Cape Town meant many tall buildings. Including the extra map, however, did not directly affect the method of delimitation.

The second modification was necessitated by the fact that central Cape Town includes three or four very long blocks which tend to intersect the CBD boundary at right angles. These blocks, Davies pointed out, decreased markedly in central business character away from their inner or CBD ends. Since they were several times as great in area as the average, roughly square city block of downtown Cape Town, and since municipal authorities were found to have base maps on which the long blocks were divided, it was decided to adopt these divisions in the CBD study. Since so few blocks were involved, this treatment probably did not greatly change the value of the results for comparisons with data from other CBDs. In fact in applying the CBI method to American cities, we find that such a modification may occasionally be desirable. Just where to draw the line in dividing such a block has generally been the greatest difficulty presented. This is the direct opposite of the difficulty encountered by Peter Scott in Australian cities where there was in many cases a plethora of named transverse lanes and avenues (see Chapter 6).

The third modification resulted from the great amount of rebuilding that was going on in central Cape Town. This is a problem often encountered in the American city where redevelopment is under way. It was not possible, Davies said, to determine the future land use since most of the lots were not yet under contract. Hence, it was decided to omit the blocks under redevelopment from the calculations. In this way calculations were based only on known facts. It was clear, however, that the rapid construction of new blocks, with most of the buildings to be tall, would require slight future shifts in the CBD boundary as subsequent land-use maps were drawn.

Although the CBI method, with the modifications suggested, was used in the actual delimitation of the CBD, boundaries based on land valuation and composite traffic were applied as additional checks. For the first of these, the 5 per cent land valuation line was used, based on 1945 valuations which were the latest available. Valuations in Cape Town are expressed as *lot* land values. These were converted to average value per block and the boundary drawn to enclose blocks with a valuation of 5 per cent or more of that of the peak value block. The second check method was based on traffic within the CBD as determined by a recent municipal survey. As with valuations, the traffic data were expressed as percentages of the peak block traffic so that comparisons with other CBDs would be possible. A boundary was drawn enclosing the blocks where visits equaled 20 per cent or more of those to the peak block.

The land valuation and composite traffic boundaries were drawn on the same map as the CBD boundary based on the CBI method. According to Davies, a satisfactory correlation was apparent between the three boundaries; in very few places were they more than a block apart. Since they were based on entirely different criteria, the boundary determined by the CBI method was considered to be generally confirmed (Fig. 5.2).

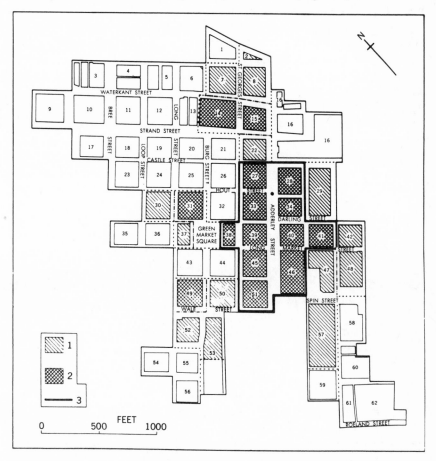

Note: The outermost boundary shown is that of the CBD as a whole. A dot marks the PLVI.

Key to legend: 1. Blocks omitted from hard core after application of exclusion rule; 2. Blocks retained under this rule; 3. Final hard core boundary.

Source: D. Hywel Davies, "The Hard Core of Cape Town's Central Business District: An Attempt at Delimitation," *Economic Geography* 36 (1960), Fig. 4.

Fig. 5.2. Extent of the CBD of Cape Town as outlined by D. Hywel Davies

The map also shows Davies' delimitation of the hard core which is discussed in this chapter. A number of blocks have been excluded because their establishments were considered atypical of the hard core on theoretical grounds. Some other blocks, namely Numbers 14, 15, 31, and 49, have been dropped because they are not part of the main contiguous mass.

According to Davies, a varying quality marked different sections of the boundary. In certain sectors the three boundaries coalesced to form a single line; in these instances he considered the CBD boundary fully acceptable. But commonly the boundary was actually a zone which lay between the divergent sections of the boundary lines. Presumably, Davies suggested, the zonal sections rather than the linear sections represent the "normal" state of affairs, and zonal boundaries would tend to be proportionately increased by plotting additional boundaries based on differing criteria. He said that it might be useful in studying any CBD to plot a number of differing boundaries on this basis and to locate and examine what might be termed "blurred" and "sharp" sections of the CBD periphery. This varying quality, he felt, might be demonstrated as resulting from the barriers to outward growth earlier described.

There is a discernible pattern of distribution of the types of CBD boundary in Cape Town. Toward the southeast is a section of linear boundary; the other three sides are essentially zonal in character. Davies pointed out the bases for the varying boundaries.

He then philosophized regarding boundary development. Generally, he said, it is regarded as "normal" for there to be few artificial barriers to outward growth; but he questions this assumption. It may well be that the presence rather than the absence of barriers is the "normal" state of affairs in the western-type CBD. This is an important question, he said, which comparative studies could answer.

At any rate, whether normal or abnormal, where there are few artificial barriers to outward growth, the CBD tends to merge gradually into a bordering zone of urban blight. There are certain spatial distributions in the CBD, according to Davies, which tend to expand more extensively and rapidly than others. The resulting positional disparity between boundaries may amount to several city blocks in width. If severe checks on the outward growth are imposed fairly near the CBD center, then these different boundaries, which may be thought of as spreading slowly outward in response to pressure being built up within the CBD, overtake one another and coalesce into a single-line boundary.

But why, Davies asks, did the southwestern side of the CBD retain a zonal boundary since it is almost as rigidly restricted as the southeast? And the northeast has retained a zonal boundary though until recently it was severely restricted by the old shoreline. He reasons that both barriers and a marked pressure outward are necessary for turning a zonal into a linear boundary, and that the CBD did not exert as much pressure for growth toward the southwest and northeast as to the southeast. Davies maintains that CBDs grow outward along arteries with the interstices lagging behind. The pressure exerted by the CBD toward the southwest and northeast has been inadequate for the purpose since such pressure is largely communicated along major arteries. These two sides have lacked arteries of first rank; hence the push necessary for formation of a linear boundary was lacking.

Expansion toward the northwest displayed most closely the "normal" characteristics of CBD growth with a zonal boundary. In this direction the CBD grew steadily through the progressive purchase of residential establishments, street by street, and their conversion to retail and other business purposes. Beyond the zonal CBD boundary lies a zone of urban blight known as the Malay Quarter. Increasing slope and a lack of through communications seem to have set a natural limit to CBD expansion in this direction even before the release of pressure through Foreshore developments.

The outline shape of the Cape Town CBD reflects the physical barriers, the block basis of calculation, and also the grid pattern of the original Dutch settlement. Davies discusses various arteries and rail developments that help to explain the course of the outline. This material is valuable for an understanding of Cape Town but more detail than is justified in this summary.

Next, Davies turns to the vertical dimension. There is the natural tendency in a western-type CBD to expand upward in response to the desire for centrality and the attraction of tall, modern office buildings. Where there are marked restrictions to normal horizontal development, as has been the case with Cape Town, such a tendency is increased. The city has a considerable number of tall buildings in proportion to the extent of its area. It would be reasonable to expect the highest blocks to occur not at the center of the CBD but near the southeastern boundary where restriction is greatest and the build-up of "pressure" at a maximum. To some extent this is true, but only general and limited conclusions are possible along these lines since new city blocks in Cape Town are artificially controlled in height by planning regulations. As far as idealized three-dimensional shape is concerned, Davies found the Cape Town CBD most nearly resembling a modified asymmetrical pyramid.

Davies introduced the time factor, too, in his consideration of the CBD. What he said in this regard contributes to an understanding of the district by tracing its evolution. There was a marked time-lag between the growth of the built-up area of Cape Town and that of the CBD, but both have been "steady and logical." The CBD's growth might be expected to have been eastwards toward the hinterland on which Cape Town has been depending more and more, but actually the growth has been chiefly toward the northwest, toward "the dead end" of Signal Hill. This assymmetry of CBD growth is regarded as a further expression of the artificial restrictions set by administrative blocks and other public blocks toward the southeast. The CBD expanded where it could, but the PLVI and the hard core of the district appear to have moved little if any. With the construction of the New National Road across the Foreshore toward the hinterlands, the PLVI may be expected to migrate, and this migration will probably be northeastward.

In a concluding section, Davies points to the essential inefficiency of Cape Town's CBD; particularly, he stresses the acute problems of vehicular and pedestrian traffic flow, aggravated by parking and commercial loading difficulties. In the original planning of the city the southwest-northeast streets were made wide and the cross streets, considered relatively unimportant, merely narrow lanes. But, with the growth of dependence upon the hinterland, rail and ultimately motor traffic entered the CBD via these cross streets which proved quite inadequate. Now a large share of the CBD's commuters and shoppers, as well as a heavy load of commercial traffic, use these cross streets and find them sadly inadequate.

The creation of the Foreshore, according to Davies, has provided the only practicable answer. One effect of the developments that are now planned will be the eventual elongation of the CBD northeastward with associated migration of the geographic center of the CBD and the PLVI. Business premises are standing empty around the southern side of the CBD while the new Foreshore area with easy access to the hinterland via the National Road is attracting more and more establishments from the present CBD. As it creeps onto the Foreshore the pressure of the CBD is being released. It is a rare city, indeed, that has such an opportunity to reorganize its CBD, but apparently few CBDs are more in need of reorganization than is Cape Town's.

Hard Core of Cape Town's CBD

In a city large enough to have a CBD of any size there is a tendency for the area immediately around the PLVI to show a concentration of those qualities that we think of particularly as characterizing the district. Compared with the average for the CBD as a whole there tend to be taller buildings, a greater concentration of central business vs. non-central business establishments, higher land values, a greater pedestrian count. This central area is the quintessence of the CBD. It is sometimes referred to as the "hard core." As one writer said, the difference between the hard core and the CBD as a whole is one of degree not of kind. The hard core is the heart of the CBD.

It would be overstatement to say that the hard core typically stands out clearly from the rest of the CBD, that its edge is easy to distinguigh. Sometimes this is true or at least the inner area of the CBD seems to rise noticeably above the rest. More often the boundary of the hard core is marked only by achievement of certain values in a gradation, requiring the somewhat arbitrary choice of some one value for marking the hard core edge.

Several people have attempted to outline the hard core. One of these was Malcolm J. Proudfoot who based his work on block-frontage-volume of sales. His "inner zone" of Philadelphia was essentially the hard core of that city (see Chapter 2). Also, Charles Downe, as pointed out earlier, delimited a hard core for Worcester, Massachusetts (see Fig. 2.2).

But it remained for D. Hywell Davies to delimit the hard core on a land-use basis and to describe his work in an article.[2] He did not start out to study the hard core. Rather, he undertook a broad study of the Cape Town CBD, the more general aspects of which were covered in the preceding resumé. The hard core study followed this broader effort.

Davies had found that the CBI method worked well for the delimitation of Cape Town's CBD. Therefore, he concluded that hard core delimitation might best be based on the same method but with "stiffer" limiting values. To be included within the hard core, it was not sufficient for a block to meet the required CBHI and CBII ratings of the CBI technique. Higher values would have to be selected.

But he did not feel that the use of higher values alone would be sufficient. He reasoned that the CBD as delimited by the CBI method included a variety of land uses some of which were atypical of the CBD. Greater "purity" of central-business land uses seemed to be desirable. So in addition to raising the index values, Davies decided to omit certain blocks characterized by such atypical uses or at least to recalculate the CBHIs and CBIIs of the blocks with these atypical uses omitted.

Among the atypical establishments were: (a) certain provincial government and municipal establishments which are not strictly central business but that, according to the CBI method, may be included under special rules (see Chapter 3). Davies felt that this special rule was too lax in the case of hard core delimitation. (b) certain establishments which appear to require less than average centrality within the CBD and are often near its edge where they benefit by more space and lower land values than are the average for the district as a whole. Where such establishments occur in the area of the hard core they might be considered atypical. Davies mentioned cinemas and hotels as examples. (c) certain lower-quality, limited-range retail establishments. Though quality, being difficult to measure, is not a criterion in the CBI method, Davies suggested that the quality of retail establishments may have to be taken into account in some way in hard core delimitation. This necessity is noticeable, he said, particularly in the case of department stores. He found that those near the PLVI offered a wide range of generally high quality goods to customers drawn

2. D. Hywel Davies, "The Hard Core of Cape Town's Central Business District: An Attempt at Delimitation," *Economic Geography* 36 (1960): 53–69.

from the entire urban agglomeration; those located near the CBD edge seemed to function largely as "suburban" stores serving lower-income residential sections of the "Zone of Urban Blight" as well as customers from more distant suburbs. Davies says that the two groups of department stores (those around the PLVI and those at the CBD edge) were found, upon field investigation, to be quite separate.

In his delimitation procedure, Davies' first step was the determination of CBHI and CBII limiting values for initial delimitation of the hard core. Since the edge of the hard core is in places visually evident because of taller buildings in the hard core, he decided to plot CBHI and CBII values against numbers of blocks to see whether some "break of slope" might be revealed which would suggest limiting values. It was apparent from the

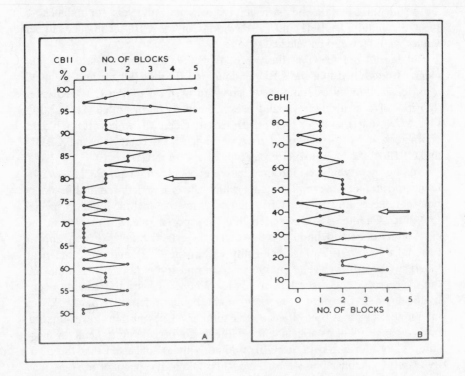

Note: These values were used in an initial delimitation of the hard core.
Source: D. Hywel Davies, "The Hard Core of Cape Town's Central Business District: An Attempt at Delimitation," *Economic Geography* 36 (1960), Fig. 1.

Fig. 5.3. "Breaks of slope" determined by plotting CBHI and CBII values against number of blocks

graphs that the boundary should be drawn where the CBHI is 4.00 and the CBII around 80 per cent (Fig. 5.3) and these values were used in an initial delimitation of the hard core. In so doing, Davies excluded isolated blocks but included blocks which, though falling short of the required values, were surrounded by included blocks. In this way a continuous boundary line was obtained.

In the resulting figure, the CBII boundary enclosed a far larger area than does the CBHI boundary. On the basis of local knowledge, Davies said, it is clear that the latter comes closer to a true delimitation. This fact suggests that the volume of CBD uses in a building, rather than the proportion of it, is critical in hard core delimitation; or possibly that the limiting CBII value of 80 per cent is too low.

In his original CBD delimitation, Davies, as an independent check, had two boundaries drawn based on other criteria, land valuation and traffic, plotting these with the boundary reached by applying the CBI method. A similar procedure was followed in the hard core delimitation except that a land valuation of 30 per cent instead of 5 per cent was used as a limiting value, and the traffic boundary was drawn on the basis of 30 per cent of the visits to the peak block instead of 20 per cent, with isolated blocks omitted to give a continuous boundary line. These two values served to delimit a hard core that correlated fairly well with that defined by the modified CBI method. This correlation suggested that the general method of delimitation must be reasonably satisfactory.

Davies' next step was an independent field check. In Cape Town the hard core makes a fairly clear visual impression which was studied in the field. Direct field observation had the advantage, too, that a few adjustments were possible based on the quality factor discussed earlier. Thus the boundary was checked carefully in the field and adjustments made to it where suggested from visual impression and local knowledge. The hard core as observed in the field was found to be smaller than that arrived at by the other means discussed, and the adjustments made as a result of direct field observations had, in general, the effect of smoothing out the boundary.

It became necessary to decide whether or not to adjust the boundary, as previously determined, to the visual impression either entirely or in part. Since both boundaries were based on land use, this decision, Davies felt, could be reached only by carefully examining the land use of each block in an attempt to detect patterns or trends that could be interpreted. Various land uses considered atypical were plotted on a map of the entire CBD which also showed the hard core as it had been determined to this point.

The blocks concerned tended to be dominated by one or more out of a list of half a dozen categories of land use. Some of these blocks were dominated by establishments that did not appear to require extreme centrality. These included cinemas, hotels, headquarters offices, and newspaper publishing and printing Davies pointed out, in each case, the bases for considering these uses atypical. And there were blocks with government and municipal offices, which are really non-CBD; and blocks largely occupied by department stores offering lower-quality goods than department stores in the vicinity of the PLVI.

Most of the blocks falling between the adjusted CBI boundary and the visual impression boundary (there were fourteen in all) were found to be largely made up of establishments which were considered atypical on theoretical grounds. This finding, Davies felt, tended to confirm the visual impression boundary and led to his conclusion that the CBHIs and CBIIs should be recalculated, counting the atypical business establishments as "X" or non-CBD for the purpose, and only for the purpose, of hard core delimitation. This was accepted as a special rule and the recalculations carried out accordingly. In his article Davies discussed the inclusion versus the exclusion of various individual blocks and arrived at a final boundary.

Davies summed up his technique of hard core delimitation as it could be applied to a CBD that has been delimited. First, the CBHI and CBII of each block is calculated according to the CBI method except that cinemas, hotels, headquarters offices, newspaper publishing and printing establishments, government and municipal offices, and "second-grade" department stores are counted as "X" or non-CBD functions in these calculations. And, second, the boundary is drawn to enclose CBD blocks with a CBHI of 4.00 or over and a CBII of 80 per cent or over with all outliers omitted but with enclosed low-value blocks counted as part of the hard core.

In most instances in the Cape Town study the technique Davies outlined could be applied objectively, but he admitted that the quality judgment used in the case of department stores is subjective. The subjectivity, he said, would operate against the use of his method in comparative studies. The obvious need, according to Davies, is for a measurable definition of quality. The question arises, too, whether the categories considered atypical in this case would prove so in other cities. Only comparative studies, he said, could answer this question.

Davies made some observations about the hard core of Cape Town as it was finally delimited (see Figure 5.2). The hard core, he said, is located asymmetrically within the CBD, being to the east and south of the geographic center. This location reflects the artificial constriction of the CBD along its southeastern boundary and the emergence on this side of major arteries leading to the main suburbs and hinterland. The hard core is small, occupying only about 16 per cent of the total area of the CBD. The core's shape, as Davies delimited it, is compact, forming a blunt cross with its major axis extending northeast-southwest along Adderly Street.

The PLVI is in the northeastern half of Cape Town's hard core (see dot, Fig. 5.2). Davies gave several possible explanations for this location. For one thing there is an isolated (and hence omitted) business area northeast of the main hard core. It could be an example of something pointed out in an earlier chapter of this book, of a tendency of the PLVI to lag behind as the CBD expands toward higher quality residential areas (in this case lying to the south) and away from railway and industrial areas that until recently lay along the sea front to the north. However, Davies went on to point out that new developments toward the northeast suggest the PLVI will move in that direction along Adderley Street.

Studies of the movement of people and vehicles within the hard core shed some further light on the situation. An analysis of peak daily visits tends to reinforce the impression that the northeastern arm of the hard core is the main area of activity. A study of vehicular flow carried out by municipal authorities further brought out the importance of the Adderly Street axis and the significance of the northeastern end of the hard core. The main value of the vehicular information, Davies said, is to demonstrate that the blunt cruciform shape of the hard core is based upon certain axes of traffic movement.

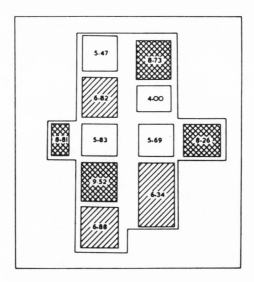

Note: The average height of each block is expressed in floors to two decimal places. Blocks with a total height index, THI, of less than 6.00 are unshaded, those from 6.00 to 8.00 diagonally shaded, and those above 8.00 are cross-hatched.

Source: D. Hywel Davies, "The Hard Core of Cape Town's Central Business District: An Attempt at Delimitation," *Economic Geography* 36 (1960), Fig. 5D.

Fig. 5.4. Total height indexes in the hard core of Cape Town

In another figure, Davies showed that, though the buildings in the hard core form the tallest major group in the city, the tallest buildings of all are not in the hard core center but near its edge (Fig. 5.4). But he explains this condition as temporary, marking the present as a transitional stage in the rebuilding of the city's CBD. The transition is also expressed, he says, in mixed nineteenth- and twentieth-century architectural styles present in the city's central areas.

6

Other Applications Abroad

The studies of Cape Town's CBD are only two of a number of downtown investigations that have been described in journals published in English. At about the same time that the work on Cape Town was under way, Peter Scott surveyed the CBDs of Australia, and in the following years B. S. Young published a study of the Port Elizabeth CBD, Harm de Blij studied Lourenço Marques, and R. J. Davies and D. S. Rajah investigated the effects of racial dualism on the Durban CBD. The work of H. Carter and G. Rowley in 1966 carried CBD research to the United Kingdom.

The Australian CBD

We shall begin with Scott's work on the Australian CBD.[1] Scott pointed out how, since the end of World War II, the larger Australian urban centers had paralleled American cities in traffic congestion and in suburban competition for retail trade. Australian business houses in the larger cities, he said, had preferred developing suburban branches rather than extending their downtown premises, and small regional shopping centers on the American pattern had been making their appearance in urban areas. At the same time, attempts had been made by municipal authorities to stem the flow of trade to the suburbs.

Yet, Scott pointed out, despite the importance of the problems rooted in the city centers, the Australian CBD had been the subject of very little geographic investigation. It was against this background that he undertook a field survey of the central areas of fourteen Australian cities, including the six state capitals. The paper discussed here was confined largely to the CBDs of the six capitals which together housed over half of Australia's population. These he delimited according to the CBI method, but his study

1. Peter Scott, "The Australian CBD," *Economic Geography* 35 (1959): 290–314.

of the individual CBD was largely confined to "an analysis of the internal ground-floor structure."

In delimiting the districts, Scott found his main problem to be that of block definition. In the delimitation method as described in Chapter 3 of this book, the rule was laid down that "a block ends only where a named street occurs." Scott had difficulty in applying this rule in his work. The centers of Melbourne and Adelaide, he said, are broken by innumerable named transverse lanes and avenues. Use of these named lanes and avenues as streets, though contrary to the original intent of the method, permitted considerable differentiation of land use, so Scott decided to accept them all as block boundaries.

The CBDs delimited tended to be elongated along dominant parallel streets and to increase in area roughly in proportion to city size (Fig. 6.1 and Table 6.1). Proportionate to population, Scott said, they are consider-

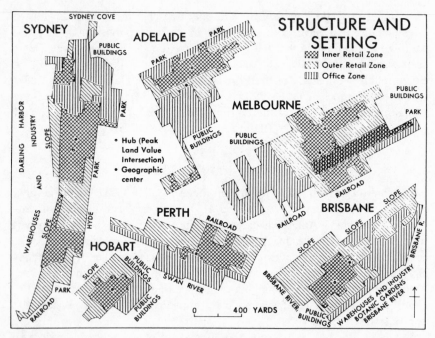

Source: Peter Scott, "The Australian CBD," *Economic Geography* 35 (1959), Fig. 2.

Fig. 6.1. Scott's study of the Australian CBD—the six state capitals

ably smaller than the American CBDs covered in the nine-city study. Sydney's CBD, in marked contrast to Melbourne's, is rigidly circumscribed by barriers. Hence, it occupies a smaller area "but has greater vertical development, more sharply differentiated land values, greater traffic conges-

Table 6.1. *Metropolitan population and CBD characteristics of the Australian state capital cities*

City	Sydney	Melbourne	Brisbane	Adelaide	Perth	Hobart
1954 population	1,863	1,524	502	484	349	95
CBD area	175	182	138	111	96	40
Distance of hub (the PLVI) from geographic center	95	210	210	150	35	95

Note: Population is in thousands, area in acres, distance in yards. From Peter Scott, "The Australian CBD," *Economic Geography* 35 (1959).

tion. . . ." (pp. 291–292) Sydney has narrower streets than Melbourne, and its traffic problems are thus much more serious. In the office quarter especially, according to Scott, street plan and building height show little organic relationship. Sydney also suffers badly from suburban competition which is favored because the CBD is so far from the geographic center of the city. In this respect it is more handicapped than any of the other cities except possibly Hobart. Brisbane's CBD, though fairly central in location, is like Sydney's in being almost wholly surrounded by natural barriers. None of the cities other than Sydney and Brisbane has barriers across its dominant axis. Only the cities with populations over one million, Sydney and Melbourne, show a marked upward growth.

Scott divided each CBD on the basis of three use types or zones—inner and outer retail zones and an office zone (see Fig. 6.1)—except an area in Melbourne that is shown as mixed (inner retail and office). Since he did not intend to calculate the areas of the zones, he simplified the boundaries where there were buffer lots with non-CBD uses. The inner zones are relatively compact and are characterized by stores selling "personal requisites" and demanding a central location. In Scott's study they are delimited according to the extent of the strongly nucleated group of department, variety, and women's clothing stores. The outer zones are characterized by stores retailing household goods and services, but, because the elements are more diverse than those of the inner zones, the outer zones are more discontinuous. Both Sydney and Adelaide have secondary inner zones, consisting mostly of low-grade stores. But whereas in Sydney the secondary nucleus lies within a continuous shopping area, in Adelaide it is cut off from the main shopping district by the office quarter. Normally, the inner zones are not exposed along the CBD edge.

Scott discussed the location of the office district relative to the retail zones in the Australian CBD, and changes going on between the position of the PLVI (which he calls "the hub") and the geographic center. Then he went on to describe and explain the distribution patterns of different types of retailing and offlces. Here he used the idea of rent theory that postulates a sequence of retail types with rent-paying ability decreasing outward from the core. Hence, Scott's analyses of central shopping districts took the form of calculating the center of gravity for the distribution of each retail type and measuring its distance from the retail node which was defined as the mean point of distribution of department stores.

Though beyond the scope of this book, these details are of interest since they help to reinforce some of the locational principles summarized in Chapter 4.[2] Scott also discussed the characteristics of "the smaller CBD," particularly as represented by Freemantle.

The CBD of Port Elizabeth

In Chapter 5, D. Hywel Davies' work on the Cape Town CBD was summarized. A year or two later another South African CBD study was published, this one dealing with Port Elizabeth, a city of some 275,000. The research and findings were described in a paper by B. S. Young[3] and are summarized here. Young followed rather closely the various steps of the original CBI delimitation technique in mapping the Port Elizabeth CBD, which he described as situated on a narrow, sloping coastal lowland strip between the steep slope of the plateau edge and the level land occupied by railway lines at the edge of Algoa Bay.

The CBD is small for the size of the city and is asymmetrical, extending to the north of the PLVI about three times as far as to the south (Fig. 6.2). Its shape reflects natural and man-made barriers to expansion. These include: the scarp at the edge of the inland plateau; railway offices, marshalling yards, and harbor facilities on the seaward side of the district; the Donkin Reserve, a preserved open space along part of the western edge of the CBD; and an area of public buildings in the south of the district. And there is an artificial limit to vertical expansion, a municipal regulation aimed at perpetuating the view seaward from the Donkin Memorial on the Reserve. Thus a vertical building limit of 104 feet prevails over practically the entire CBD.

As part of the research project, land-use regions were outlined for the Port Elizabeth CBD. The regional zonal pattern Young arrived at took both ground-floor uses and uses on other floors into account. The method of arriving at the regions involved the following steps: (1) plotting ground-floor uses lot by lot on a base map; (2) plotting over the ground-floor uses the dominant land use of the other floors of each lot; (3) arriving at a number of reasonably homogeneous land-use regions from the resulting intricate mosaic; (4) plotting on the base map with symbols the locations of certain specific land uses, including transportation offices, cinemas, furniture and household stores, clothing shops, department-variety stores, auto-

2. For a further discussion of some of these points see Peter Scott, *Geography and Retailing* (Chicago: Aldine · Atherton, 1970).

3. B. S. Young, "Aspects of the Central Business District of Port Elizabeth, Cape Province," *Journal for Social Research* 12, no. 1 (May 1961): 27–48.

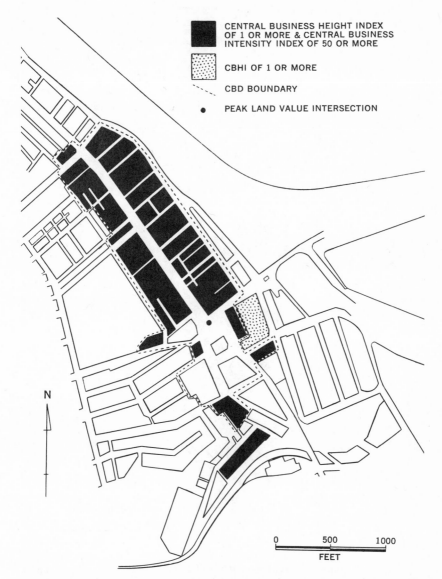

CENTRAL BUSINESS HEIGHT INDEX
OF 1 OR MORE & CENTRAL BUSINESS
INTENSITY INDEX OF 50 OR MORE

CBHI OF 1 OR MORE

CBD BOUNDARY

● PEAK LAND VALUE INTERSECTION

N

0   500   1000
FEET

Source: B. S. Young, "Aspects of the Central Business District of Port Elizabeth, Cape Province," *Journal for Social Research,* May, 1961, Fig. 2. Reproduced with permission of the Human Sciences Research Council.

Fig. 6.2. The CBD of Port Elizabeth as delineated on the basis of blocks according to the CBI method

motive service establishments, hotels, banks, building societies, and several others, thus confirming the regions earlier outlined; (5) identifying distinctive zones on the basis of the relative concentrations of land uses and their positions within the CBD.

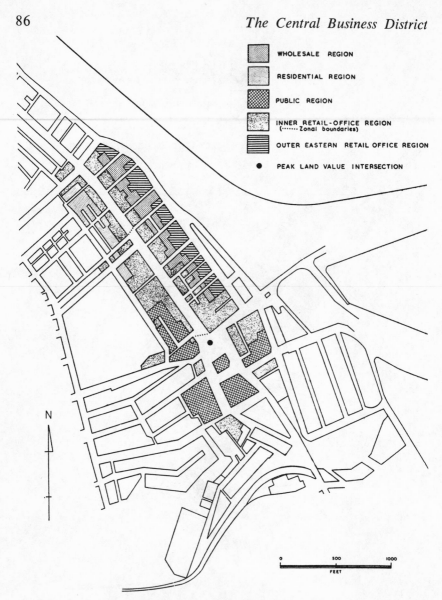

WHOLESALE REGION

RESIDENTIAL REGION

PUBLIC REGION

INNER RETAIL-OFFICE REGION
(······ Zonal boundaries)

OUTER EASTERN RETAIL OFFICE REGION

● PEAK LAND VALUE INTERSECTION

N

Source: B. S. Young, "Aspects of the Central Business District of Port Elizabeth, Cape Province," *Journal for Social Research,* May, 1961, Fig. 7. Reproduced with permission of the Human Sciences Research Council.

Fig. 6.3. Land-use regions of the Port Elizabeth CBD

Young continued with an analysis of the land-use picture (Fig. 6.3). The heart of the CBD is the inner retail-office region which is divided into a central zone, a northern zone, and a southern zone. On the east side of Main Street (the major north-south street) most retail establishments reflect the narrow, eastward-sloping lowland site by occupying basements which emerge lower down the seaward slopes as ground floors.

The presence of a wholesale region is not in accord with the situation in the average American CBD where wholesaling, at least where the merchandise is kept on the premises, is not regarded as a central business use. Its occurrence in the Port Elizabeth CBD seems to be explained, in part at least, by the presence of cheap land not very well situated for retailing. "Requiring no frontage on the main arteries of pedestrian and vehicular flow in order to pursue their business, the wholesale concerns are located in nearby backwaters where land values are relatively low." (p. 36)

A particularly interesting feature in Port Elizabeth is the presence of an outlying business area that Young calls "a non-central business district." It lies about a mile northwest of the northern boundary of the main district (Fig. 6.4). The non-central business district, he says, should not be confused with neighborhood or suburban shopping centers. It offers services equal in miniature to those offered by the CBD and in some respects excelling them. At present it does not form a coherent related whole; and storage, wholesaling, and some industry are found along the main street. But there is, he thinks, enough central business, retail and office, to justify designating the area as a central business district. There are more garages and automotive showrooms than in the CBD, three large banks, two large department stores (not represented in the CBD), and a number of office blocks tenanted by lawyers, doctors, wool brokers, and other business of a central nature. As Young says, "The Law Courts and Municipal Market— both migrants from the central area of the CBD—could well form the nucleus of a very important outlying business district in Port Elizabeth." (p. 34)

At any rate this non-central business district or secondary CBD or whatever we choose to call it is an interesting phenomenon. In some ways it corresponds to Proudfoot's "outlying business center,"[4] though the latter seems to be more consistently second-level, less competitive with the regular CBD. Young explains his secondary CBD as due to proximity to industrial concerns in the northern areas of Port Elizabeth; lower land values than in the main CBD; greater availability of building space with more level sites; and ease of parking and of access from main residential areas (see Fig. 6.4). Locations of the two districts in relation to the main industrial and residential routes into the city help to explain the existence of the non-central CBD.

Applying the CBI Technique to Lourenço Marques

A CBD that was found to present some interesting problems in applying the CBI technique was described by Harm de Blij.[5] In his paper on Lour-

4. Malcolm J. Proudfoot, "City Retail Structure," *Economic Geography* 13 (1937): 425–428.

5. Harm J. de Blij, "The Functional Structure and Central Business District of Lourenço Marques, Moçambique," *Economic Geography* 38 (1962): 56–77.

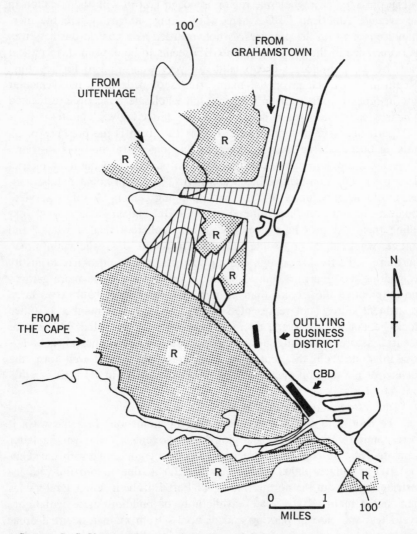

100′

FROM
GRAHAMSTOWN

FROM
UITENHAGE

R

R

R

R

FROM
THE CAPE

R

OUTLYING
BUSINESS
DISTRICT

N

CBD

R

R

R

0   1
MILES

100′

Source: B. S. Young, "Aspects of the Central Business District of Port Elizabeth,
Cape Province," *Journal for Social Research,* May, 1961, Fig. 5. Reproduced with
permission of the Human Sciences Research Council.

*Fig. 6.4. The relative positions of the CBD and the outlying business district in
Port Elizabeth*

enço Marques, he first discussed the history of settlement on Delagoa Bay
and then went into some detail regarding the city's functions. But it is his
discussion of "core and central business district" that concerns us chiefly
here. Particularly, he points out the problems of applying a technique such
as the CBI method to the Lourenço Marques situation even though the city

has a population of some 100,000 to 200,000 and is thus in the same size range as the nine United States CBDs that were studied comparatively.

One of de Blij's prime difficulties was that the CBI technique begins with the PLVI, thus assuming areal variations in land values. But in Lourenço Marques such differences do not exist. Land in the "central section," which he says is a rather arbitrarily defined region, is assumed to be of uniform value. The buyer's choice, he adds, is based on location rather than price.

Although vertical development in the core area is considerable, upper floors are rarely used for retailing. They are occupied by living quarters, and only three real office buildings exist in the city.

Another difficulty in using something like the CBI method for delimiting the CBD is that the blocks of much of the central city are large, rather like those that characterize Salt Lake City's CBD. According to de Blij, "The central section of such a block is an area of open storage, parking, or nondescript sheds and shacks." (p. 64) Stores extend varying distances into this central empty area so floor space measurements are unreliable.

Because of such problems, de Blij based his delimitation on the frontage occupied by retail establishments including banks. A percentage for each block was derived on this basis and a frequency diagram used to decide on breaks in intensity so a map could be made showing varying intensities by blocks.

Lourenço Marques resembles Cape Town, de Blij says, in that it has an area of reclaimed flat land into which the CBD will be able to expand. But the CBD of Lourenço Marques is much less congested.

The Ethnic Factor and Durban's Two CBDs

Some CBD patterns are based in considerable part upon cultural influences. Such patterns are well illustrated by the Durban CBD.

Durban is almost as large as Cape Town, and since both are multiracial it might be expected that their CBDs would be very similar. But there are some interesting contrasts based on ethnic differences that are brought out in the process of CBD delimitation. In Cape Town, where CBD services are overwhelmingly under the control of Whites, D. H. Davies applied the CBI method of CBD delimitation with very little trouble, but R. J. Davies and D. S. Rajah, working in Durban, encountered some interesting "complexities" in using the technique.[6]

These differences seem to have arisen from the independent participation in and control of CBD services by two racially, economically, and socially distinct population groups in Durban—Whites and Indians. CBD services controlled by the two groups have been subject to spatial segre-

6. R. J. Davies and D. S. Rajah, "The Durban CBD: Boundary Delimitation and Racial Dualism," *The South African Geographical Journal* 47 (December 1965): 45–58.

gation processes arising from ethnic-cultural differences between the groups and from legislative controls exercised over the spatial distribution of Indian trade.

In Durban two distinct and segregated central area trading communities in juxtaposition have resulted. They are not only racially and socially distinct but they also show marked differences in internal functional composition. Land uses, for example, which in the White-dominated sector would be considered non-central business, in the Indian sector appear to fulfill functions which in that setting are essentially central business. To some degree the pattern is more what one would expect in an Asiatic city than in an American city. Davies and Rajah concentrated particularly on the special delimitation problems that resulted.

Fundamental to the contrast between the CBDs of Cape Town and Durban is the contrast between the non-White populations of the two cities (Table 6.2). Even more important than the actual numbers, however, are

Table 6.2. *Urban population comparison by race for Durban and Cape Town economic regions, 1960*

Race	Cape Town %	Durban %
White	38.1	29.5
Coloured	52.2	4.1
Indian	1.1	35.5
African	8.6	30.9
	100.0	100.0

Source: R. J. Davies and D. S. Rajah, "The Durban CBD: Boundary Delimitation and Racial Dualism," *South African Geographical Journal* 47 (1965).

their roles in CBD activities. In Durban, Indians participate in CBD activities to a much greater degree than do the Coloureds in Cape Town, and they occupy significantly larger proportions of the positions of management and control.

In their CBD research, Davies and Rajah used Central Durban as their "study frame" (Fig. 6.5). The frame, which covers the area of earliest settlement in Durban, was not scientifically delimited by Davies and Rajah but "covers the well marked historical entity of Central Durban" and is the portion of the city "within which the CBD may be expected to lie." (p. 48) (In Chapter 3 of this book a somewhat similar area was designated for mapping in CBD delimitation: the land around the PLVI that might be called the obvious CBD plus a sufficiently wide belt beyond to include any land that might conceivably fall within the district.)

Within the frame, Davies and Rajah say, a pattern of segregation of land ownership between Whites and Indians has persisted since the late nineteenth century and has been the basis for a dual trading community. The

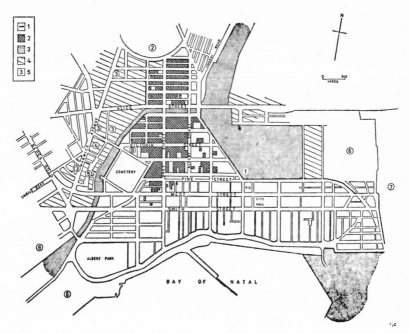

Key to legend: 1. Study frame boundary; 2. Indian owned land within the frame; 3. Railway and harbor land; 4. Zone of public and semi-public land uses; 5. (1) Central railway station, (2) Greyville race course, (3) Non-white central city bus terminal, (4) Indian squatters' market, (5) White retail and wholesale markets, (6) Industrial areas, (7) Resort region, (8) Indian market.

Source: Davies and Rajah, "The Durban CBD: Boundary Delimitation and Racial Dualism," *South African Geographical Journal* 47 (December 1965), Fig. 1.

Fig. 6.5. The study frame of central Durban

area's total resident population in 1960 was 4.39 per cent of the total population of Durban. Of this number, 47.67 per cent were White and 37.11 per cent Indian.

To a considerable degree the two groups occupy distinct areas. White ownership and occupation of the land is concentrated chiefly in the city blocks south of Pine Street. The Indians are located essentially north of Pine Street and west of Albert. This area contains 99 per cent of the Indian population of the frame.

The ethnic pattern of the frame, the authors say, originated mainly after 1870, when increasing numbers of poor Indian workers released from indentures on sugar estates together with immigrant traders began establishing shops and shack settlements on the swampy land on the northern periphery of the evolving White CBD that was focused on central West Street. As Indian trade and residence expanded southward and eastward they began to impinge upon the edges of the White CBD which was expanding

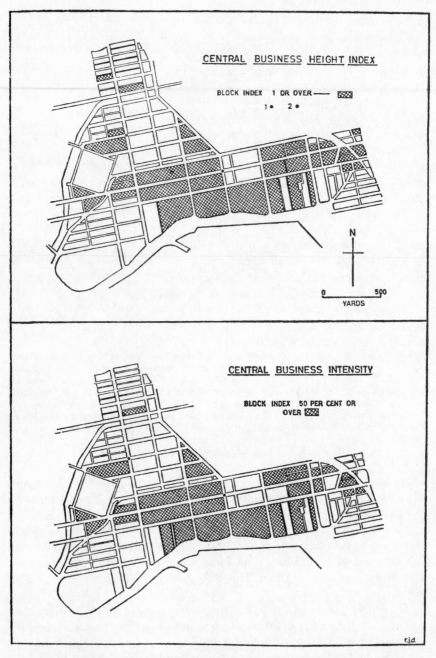

CENTRAL BUSINESS HEIGHT INDEX

BLOCK INDEX 1 OR OVER ——— ▨
1 • 2 •

N

0   500
YARDS

CENTRAL BUSINESS INTENSITY

BLOCK INDEX 50 PER CENT OR OVER ▨

r.j.d.

1. PLVI of White sector, black dot; 2. PLVI of Indian sector, small circle.
Source: Davies and Rajah, "The Durban CBD: Boundary Delimitation and Racial Dualism," *South African Geographical Journal* 47 (December 1965), Fig. 2.

Fig. 6.6. Indexes resulting from application of the CBI technique to Durban with no adjustments

outward from the core. Friction resulted from trade competition between the two groups, from the Indians acquiring land and buildings, and from a clash of the two cultures. Under a Colonial Act of 1897, trade licensing authorities were granted powers over issuance of new licenses. This action could not stop existing Indian trade, but it has in recent years prevented further diffusion within the central area and has tended to concentrate further Indian trade development within the area already dominated by the Indians.

When the CBI technique was applied to Durban it was found to be satisfactory for definition of what may be termed the White CBD (Fig. 6.6). But it did not allow for the emergence of an Indian sector in the CBD structure.

The White CBD as delimited is broadly rectangular and is symmetrically arranged around a PLVI. Its boundary and shape are governed by the desirability of frontages on Durban's two main streets, on the one hand, and by physical and man-made barriers to expansion on the other. These factors have encouraged an elongated, east to west, shape. Zonal boundaries separate the CBD from a White apartment area on the southwest and a holiday resort region on the east. And a zonal boundary separates the White CBD from a developing Indian trading center on the north. This boundary represents a zone of rejection by White entrepreneurs reluctant to move toward the Indian business center. By virtue of the licensing controls mentioned earlier, the zone is also the limit to which Indian trade is able to encroach on the White CBD.

Why does the standard procedure of the CBI method fail to distinguish an Indian CBD sector which we know exists? (See Fig. 6.6.) Davies and Rajah suggest two possible hypotheses: (1) That the frame blocks dominantly occupied by Indians and containing Indian CBD services but not reaching the required index levels are part of a normal gradient of CBD services in a transition zone between strictly CBD and strictly residential areas. According to the authors, field inspection suggests that such mixed-use areas are typical. (2) An alternative possibility is that the index levels used in the CBI method are not sufficiently sensitive to the ecology and perhaps abnormal (in a western sense) dichotomy which appears to exist between CBD uses and non-central business uses in the Indian-dominated blocks.

There is considerable evidence in favor of the second hypothesis. Field observation and interviews with local tradesmen and planning authorities suggest that an Indian CBD sector does exist and that it merits definition as part of the overall CBD structure. The existence of two separate peak land-value intersections, one in the White and the other in the Indian sector, suggest that it may be possible to postulate a separate Indian CBD as distinct from an additional zone of the already defined White CBD.

The authors considered various factors that might be involved in the possible delimitation of an Indian CBD. A grid pattern of streets and city blocks extends through both White and Indian sectors of the frame, and the buildings which house CBD services and other functions in the Indian sector are essentially western in concept though more modest and older

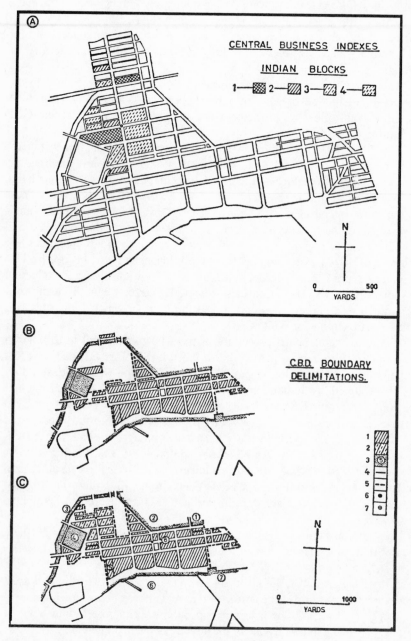

Fig. 6.7. Illustrations of procedures used in adapting the CBI delimitation technique to Durban conditions

than those of the White sector. It follows that the basic field and analysis techniques of the CBI method should be about as applicable to the Indian sector as to the White sector. But it is important to realize that the western framework has been subject to a good deal of modification through ethnic-cultural processes, the direct and indirect influences of segregation, and other factors, which, in combination, have had a marked influence on land use and on socio-economic functions.

The authors point out that there is a major characteristic of land-use composition of the blocks within the Indian sector which may go far to explain their relatively low index values. This is the abnormally high proportion of residential land and organizational land, the latter including schools and cultural organizations but little government use. This land-use combination is explained by these points: (1) A dichotomy of trade and residence typical of an indigenous Indian city is likely to occur in Durban. (2) The shortage of residential land for Indian occupation within a reasonable distance of the city center (together with legislative controls since 1943) has encouraged residential concentration in the frame. (3) The concentration of residences may represent a persistence of the pattern of first immigrant settlement restricted in expansion by resistance offered by surrounding White residential areas. (4) The growth of Indian cultural orgnizations in the frame is a concomitant of Indian residential development and may spur more such development. (5) The present level of Indian CBD services is immature in comparison to that reached by the Whites. It is a stage in the evolution toward a fully developed CBD in the western sense. Office, business, and professional services are little represented; investment money has gone more to residential blocks built above stores.

Davies and Rajah reached the conclusion that the CBI method is satisfactory within the Indian sector, but they felt that an adjustment of the statistical levels of the indexes was necessary to accomodate the conditions prevalent in that sector. They suggested the following four steps (Fig. 6.7):

Step 1. The city block southwest of the PLVI within the Indian sector

---

(A) Indian sector delimitation with cartographic representation of Steps 1 through 4. (B) The CBD boundary delimitation by the standard Murphy and Vance index method. (C) The CBD as finally delimited including a White and an Indian sector. Key to legend for 4B and 4C: 1. CBD blocks with CBII of over 50% and CBHI of over 1 in Figure 4B, and comprising the White CBD sector in Figure 4C. 2. The Indian CBD sector in Figure 4C. 3. Barriers to the lateral expansion of the CBD as follows: (1) Gaol; (2) Railway land and station yards; (3) Belt of public and semi-public land uses and the main line of railway; (4) West Street Cemetery; (5) The Legal Center; (6) Bay foreshore; (7) Harbor lands; (8) The Civic Government center. 4. Linear CBD boundaries. 5. Zonal CBD boundaries. 6. PLVI (White sector). 7. PLVI (Indian sector).

Source: Davies and Rajah, "The Durban CBD: Boundary Delimitation and Racial Dualism," *South African Geographical Journal* 47 (December 1965), Fig. 4.

qualified under the accepted standards of the CBI method. It is assumed
to represent the core of the Indian CBD sector.

Step 2. By plotting the cumulative frequency of blocks against intervals of
CBII values, it is possible to identify a break in slope at the 40-50 per cent
and over level (Fig. 6.8). A similar graph plotted for CBHI levels
identified a break in slope at the 0.6 CBHI level.

Step 3. Assuming that these breaks represent significant limits within the
CBD frame, the boundary may be drawn to include all contiguous blocks
that have a CBII of 40 per cent or more and a CBHI of 0.6 or more. Thus
the two ranks of blocks have been identified as belonging to the Indian
CBD.

Step 4. A third rank of CBD blocks may be identified if the tendency for
residential uses especially on upper floors is taken into account. All blocks
with a CBII of 50 per cent or more on the ground floor and with a CBHI
of 0.6 or more were identified and included within the Indian CBD sector
boundary.

As a result of application of the foregoing rules the irregularly shaped
Indian sector of the CBD was found to enclose ten contiguous blocks (see
Fig. 6.7). The sector extends along the north-south axis of Grey Street,
traditionally the main street of Indian trade (see Fig. 6.5). Davies and

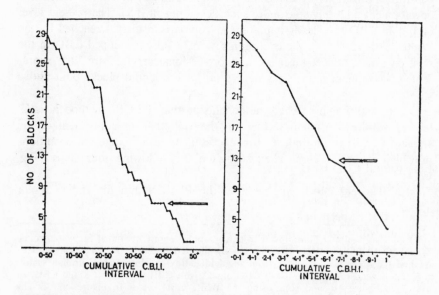

Note: Arrows indicate suggested breaks of slope.
Source: Davies and Rajah, "The Durban CBD: Boundary Delimitation and Racial
Dualism," *South African Geographical Journal* 47 (December 1965), Fig. 3.

*Fig. 6.8. Indian CBD Sector Delimitation Step 2—numbers of frame blocks
plotted against cumulative CBI and CBH index intervals*

Rajah discuss various characteristics of the Indian CBD sector and the possibilities of its expansion, which lie chiefly toward the north.

In their conclusion the authors point out that their technique has been applied to just one city and that only studies of other cities of similar character will serve to verify or modify the suggested weighting of the indexes.

Davies and Rajah criticize their own study in pointing out that it is based on an analysis framework which is essentially western in physical context. Thus the Indian CBD sector appears as a modification of a western CBD structure rather than a direct transplant of the intricate diffusion and complexity of land use and socio-economic functions characteristic of the distinctly non-western portion of an indigenous Indian city. The authors doubted if the suggested methods would be applicable to such a city.

Davies and Rajah suggest the need for more research into a variety of problems related to their study. These may be listed as follows:

(1) The exact ecological relationships between central business and non-central business uses within the Indian sector, and particularly the type of relationship that exists between place of work and place of residence.

(2) The stage of development of the CBD and its relationships to the stage of economic and social development of the Indian and other non-White communities it serves.

(3) Differences in types of CBD uses which may arise from differences in demand from non-White and White communities.

(4) Avenues of central business investment available to Indian entrepreneurs.

The CBD of Cardiff

The latest published CBD analysis that will be discussed is a case study of the Cardiff CBD by H. Carter and G. Rowley.[7] Unlike the other studies presented in this and the preceding chapter, the work on Cardiff was not based primarily on the CBI technique. Nevertheless, it is sufficiently like them in other respects that it is summarized here.

Cardiff, with a population of 265,270 in 1961, is a little larger than the average of the nine cities whose CBDs formed the basis for the generalizations of Chapter 4 but only about one-third as large as Cape Town. This study of Cardiff's central area is of particular interest since the city is old as compared with American, Australian, and South African cities. Its age causes Cardiff's CBD to differ greatly from its American counterparts, and from those of the other cities discussed.

7. H. Carter and G. Rowley, "The Morphology of the Central Business District of Cardiff," *Institute of British Geographers, Transactions*, no. 38 (1966): pp. 119–134.

Carter and Rowley, in their work, first sought a general but objective method of CBD delimitation. Armed with such a technique they hoped to measure shape, area, and internal composition and to relate these with variables such as city population, rate of population and housing increase, and economic funcitions; in this way they hoped to arrive at some generalizations regarding the nature of the CBD. They point out, however, that the very idea of attempting to outline and define the district, which is the purpose of delimitation, is subject to criticism since, obviously, a precise outline of the CBD does not exist in reality. It "is a product," they say, "not of the nature of the CBD, but of the technique of definition." (p. 119) The question is raised here, however, whether it would not be better to say that both factors are involved.

Another interesting and basic point made by Carter and Rowley is that the concept of the CBD has come into being in the present century largely because the physical reality of this central area is the product not only of the rapid urban expansion of the last hundred years but also of a complex process of internal reorganization. In Western Europe, contemporary forces are not operating in a vacuum; they are brought to bear on an urban fabric long in existence. In contrasting the problems of CBD delimitation of Western Europe with those of America, it is well to keep this depth of historic background in mind.

Two elements of site were important in the growth of Cardiff. The first was a glacial terrace which afforded a well-drained area with the possibility of constructing good clean wells. This terrace, lying east of the River Taff, provided easy access to the river, a dry causeway which facilitated construction of a bridge. The second site element was a break in the profile of the River Taff which made Cardiff the head of navigation, the point where the river met tidal water. The street layout of Cardiff was controlled by the terrace. One axis followed it, parallel to the river; this was St. Mary Street. The main east-west route joined the axis at the castle, giving the town a "T" shape.

The initial establishment of the Norman castle and town dates from the eleventh century. By the mid-nineteenth century, central Cardiff was surrounded on all sides by marked physical barriers. To the north lay the castle and its protected land, to the south the South Wales Railway, to the west the river and its marshy lowland, to the east successive lines of wall and canal, dock feeder, and Taff Valley Railway. The subsequent increase of population, from 10,000 in 1841 to 250,000 in 1961, brought immense pressures on this central area, but the boundaries remain as significant constricting features. And out of the external pressures being exerted and of the squeeze within these boundaries the urban zones of Cardiff emerged.

Carter and Rowley decided, as Murphy and Vance had done, that landuse data provided the most satisfactory criteria for CBD delimitation. Accordingly, in their work on the CBD of Cardiff, land use was surveyed

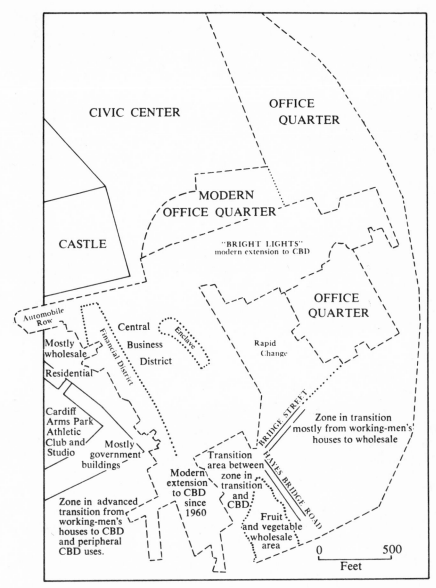

CIVIC CENTER

OFFICE QUARTER

MODERN OFFICE QUARTER

"BRIGHT LIGHTS" modern extension to CBD

CASTLE

OFFICE QUARTER

Automobile Row

Central Business District

Financial District

Enclave

Rapid Change

Mostly wholesale

Residential

Cardiff Arms Park Athletic Club and Studio

Mostly government buildings

Modern extension to CBD since 1960

Transition area between zone in transition and CBD

BRIDGE STREET

HAYES BRIDGE ROAD

Zone in transition mostly from working-men's houses to wholesale

Zone in advanced transition from working-men's houses to CBD and peripheral CBD uses.

Fruit and vegetable wholesale area

0   500
Feet

Source: H. Carter and G. Rowley, "The Central Business District of Cardiff," *Institute of British Geographers, Transactions* no. 38, 1966, pp. 119–134, Fig. 8.

Fig. 6.9. Urban regions in central Cardiff

for an area that included all land that could possibly be considered as within the CBD, and upper floors as well as ground were mapped. CBD use was defined as retailing of goods and services for profit. Floor-space indexes were derived; chiefly use was made of a ratio of floor space to ground-floor space or to the area of the plot on which the building stood.

A ratio of 2 or more, though it amounted chiefly to a height index, was considered significant in outlining the CBD. In a general way it marked the contiguous area of CBD but was checked against the three land-use maps.

Here the nature of the town became important. Carter and Rowley point out that the central area of the British urban center emerged from a long process of fluctuating growth which seldom in British towns has produced a uniform block pattern. They felt that over-generalization and loss of precision would be inevitable if they used blocks as was done in applying the CBI method to American cities.

They proceeded then to investigate land values for the central area and made maps on this basis. As they point out, "It is, however, dangerous to count these values as objective for they are only the assessments of the valuation officer and no more. . . ." (p. 123)

Because no one of the techniques of definition available proved adequate for the work on Cardiff, " . . . interpretation and rationalization into 'urban regions' was carried out using no single criterion or combination of criteria." (pp. 124–125) Various lines of evidence were used; for example, in some cases shop customers were studied to see to what extent the shops attracted customers from outside the city. This was considered to be the *true* CBD association.

A map of urban regions that illustrated the Carter and Rowley study shows additional characteristics of their approach (Fig. 6.9). According to the authors, the theories of Burgess and Hoyt have been reflected in the growth pattern of the Cardiff CBD.

The methods used by Carter and Rowley undoubtedly led to a depth of understanding of the central area of a city; this fact is made clear in the remainder of the study, in which much information is given regarding the evolution and characteristics of central Cardiff. The authors point out in conclusion that in Europe where every central area is the product of a long evolutionary process there is danger in lifting out of context arbitrarily-defined parts of cities. In the interrelations of all parts, they say, there is still a useful field of study. It should be pointed out, however, that methods such as those used in this study of the Cardiff CBD cannot be expected to provide objectively comparable areas for different cities.

7

The Census Bureau's CBD

This book presents several concepts but inevitably some play larger roles than others. The preceding four chapters have been built largely around the CBD concept of Murphy and Vance. The present chapter will treat a CBD concept developed and used by the United States Bureau of the Census. By the very prestige of the Bureau's sponsorship, if for no other reason, this idea was destined to become widely known and used. There is also a brief assessment in this chapter of research based on the Census Bureau's CBDs.

Introducing the Concept

The U. S. Bureau of the Census had not officially outlined central business districts prior to 1954. In fact, officials of the Bureau did not address themselves seriously to the problem of outlining CBDs until the early 1950s. But some sort of area had to be outlined before the Bureau could fulfill the growing local demand for collected business statistics for the central, and what appeared to be the busiest, area of each city. How should such areas be delimited? At one point the CBI technique was considered by the Bureau, but it would have required a great deal of field work. Something simpler was needed.

The Bureau decided to base its central business district system upon census tracts. Under the sponsorship of local census tract committees, tracts had been outlined for most cities of 50,000 or more and in many instances for whole standard metropolitan statistical areas. Since the census tract concept is basic to the Bureau's method of outlining central business districts, a brief explanation of census tracts is in order.

According to the U. S. Bureau of the Census, census tracts are small areas into which large cities and metropolitan areas have been divided for statistical purposes. They should be approximately equal in population, containing between 2,500 and 8,000 persons each, and ideally averaging about 4,000 residents. Each census tract is made up of census enumeration districts which must be bounded by easily recognizable lines since census enumerators have to be able to identify the boundaries in the field. Hence, census tract boundaries follow streets, highways, railroads, rivers, canals, and the like, or reasonably permanent political lines. Features that form major barriers—a cliff or other steep slope, a broad river, or a major arterial—make good tract boundaries. The tract outlines are intended to be as permanent as possible so that the tracts will be comparable areas over a long period of time.

A basic attempt is made to enclose in each tract an area that is as homogeneous as possible in population characteristics, such as race, national origins, economic status, and living conditions. But since it is impossible completely to meet all the desired criteria, the pattern of census tracts into which the average city is divided normally is arrived at by compromises. The actual work of outlining the tracts may be done by the city planning department or other individuals under the supervision of the local census tract committee, but the results are subject to Census Bureau approval.

The foregoing is only a brief introduction to census tracts; much more detail is available in the latest *Census Tract Manual* of the Bureau of the Census; but enough has been said to give the reader some background for judging the advantages and drawbacks of the Census Bureau's CBD concept.

It was necessary for the Bureau of the Census to arrange for the delineation of "central business districts" before a program of tabulating census business data for the districts could be implemented. This delineation was accomplished in time for the 1954 Census of Business through cooperation of the census tract committees in cities included in the CBD program. These committees in turn had the help of a variety of local interests, such as business firms and associations, newspapers, planning agencies, welfare organizations, local government bodies, etc.

The Director of the Census Bureau, in a letter to the census tract committees, stated that the objective in defining a CBD was "to provide a basis for comparing changes in business activity in the central business district with those in the remainder of the metropolitan area of the central city." Since there were no generally accepted rules for determining what a central business district area should include or exclude, the Census Bureau (1) provided a general characterization of the central business district as "an area of very high land valuation; an area characterized by a high concentration of retail businesses, offices, theaters, hotels, and 'service' businesses; and an area of high traffic flow"; and (2) required that the CBD ordinarily should be defined to follow existing tract lines; that is, it should consist of one or more whole census tracts.

It was recognized that the tract basis for CBDs might lead to the inclusion of area segments that did not meet the first criterion or to the exclusion of small segments that did. Provision was made, however, for splitting tracts where a serious problem was encountered. The use of tract lines for boundaries also was consistent with the desire to keep Census CBD boundaries constant in order to maximize the value of comparisons over time. In some cities, previously established CBDs, or similar areas which substantially corresponded to the Census Bureau's requirements for CBDs, were accepted for use in the program. Where the CBD designated by the local committee as their central business district consisted of a new, single tract, it did not have to adhere strictly to the population limits ordinarily set for tracts. Thus it might have less than the 2,500 inhabitants normally set as the minimum. But, ordinarily, existing tracts sufficed.

It may be assumed that in each city, at least each city of 100,000 or more, the local census tract committee and its advisors went to work armed with the foregoing directives or suggestions. They held meetings and arrived, in each case, at a decision as to the tract or combination of tracts that in their combined judgment best represented their city's CBD. The method amounted to a case of applying the techniques of perception within the limits of a framework of census tracts (see Chapter 2). The areas outlined have specific values and limitations. In view of the distinctiveness of the concept, each such unit will be referred to as a Census CBD throughout the rest of this book.

In 1958, Census CBD data were published in Central Business District Statistics bulletins for most United States cities; for 1963 and later, Census CBD data were published in Major Retail Centers bulletins. A distinction needs to be made between Census CBDs and Major Retail Centers (MRCs). A Census CBD is a type of MRC. It is just one, though of course the major one, of the MRCs of the particular urban area. MRCs (other than the CBD) are commonly defined as those concentrations of retail stores (located inside the Standard Metropolitan Statistical Areas [SMSAs] but outside the Census CBDs themselves) which include a major general merchandise store, usually a department store. But our concern is with the Census CBD rather than with MRCs in general.

The information made available for Census CBDs in MRC bulletins has to do with retailing. Data are given on the number of establishments, sales, payroll, and paid employees for retail stores in total and for the following ten groups: (1) building materials, hardware, and farm equipment dealers; (2) general merchandise group stores; (3) food stores; (4) automotive dealers; (5) gasoline service stations; (6) apparel and accessory stores; (7) furniture, home furnishings, and equipment stores; (8) eating and drinking places; (9) drug stores and proprietary stores; and (10) miscellaneous retail stores. The data are for the Census CBD, but similar information is summed up in companion tables for the corporate city and for the SMSA. Data are given for 1963 as well as for 1967 and analyzed on a percentage basis for 1967. Finally, in a table, the individual MRCs of the SMSA (other than the CBD) are analyzed.

The map equipment is largely standardized. One page of the 1967

Census of Business, "Major Retail Centers in Standard Metropolitan Statistical Areas, Pennsylvania," for example, shows the Pittsburgh SMSA and the corporate city of Pittsburgh on one scale, and the Census CBD on a much larger scale (Fig. 7.1). Though for smaller cities the maps shown ordinarily are for 1967 only, for Pittsburgh and other cities of its magnitude a comparable 1963 map is included as well. Another map page shows the corporate city of Pittsburgh, the Census CBD (as a dot on the map), the inner portions of the SMSA, and the MRCs of the urban area (Fig. 7.2).

Census CBD data, like other Census of Business data, are subject to the disclosure rule which, in effect, says that no data can be published which disclose the operations of an individual establishment or business organization. Hence, some items have to be withheld. Fortunately, however, the number of establishments in a kind of business is not considered a disclosure so that this may appear in instances where other items of information for the same kind of business or locality are withheld.

Research Use of the Census Bureau's CBDs

Publication of the Census CBD statistics for 1954, and later for 1958, 1963, and 1967, opened the door for several research investigations. Regression analysis has been involved in most cases, but this book is concerned with the lines of inquiry and in possible findings rather than in details of statistical techniques. Four studies will be summarized briefly to illustrate the research value of the Census CBD data.

CBD RETAIL SALES TRENDS AND CITY SIZE

Edgar Horwood and Ronald Boyce, in their book published in 1959, devoted a chapter to "Central Retail Sales Trends and City Size, 1948–1954."[1] In this chapter they attempted "to determine the relative change in the status of [Census] CBD retail sales . . . over a given period and to develop generalizations concerning the characteristics of each activity in relation to city size." (p. 28) Thus they were particularly concerned with the "per capita rate of change in retail sales . . . in relation to urbanized area population," (p. 28) with whether a predictable relationship existed.

They used Census Bureau retail sales data obtained for 69 cities for 1948 and 1954, but admitted the data had two major limitations. First, the Census CBD is not precisely defined by the Bureau; and, second, 1950 population figures had to be used with both 1948 and 1954 Census CBD sales data. Since U. S. Census population data are available only for every tenth year, the use of 1950 figures was a necessity. However, the authors

---

1. Edgar M. Horwood and Ronald R. Boyce, *Studies of the Central Business District and Urban Freeway Development* (Seattle: University of Washington Press, 1959), Chapter 3.

PITTSBURGH, PA.
Standard Metropolitan Statistical Area
and Central Business District
1967

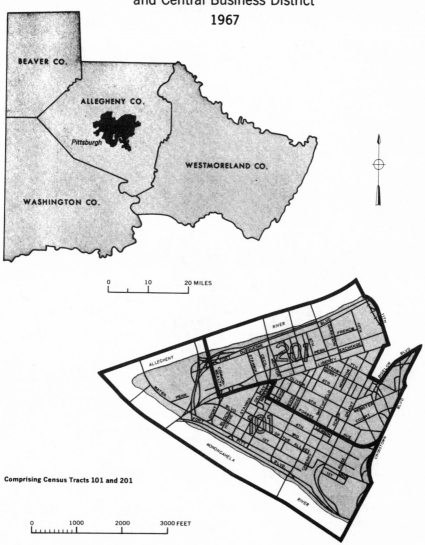

Fig. 7.1. First map page for Pittsburgh, Pa., in Major Retail Centers bulletin of the 1967 Census of Business

introduced a method of correction which they say compensates somewhat for this population data limitation.

Horwood and Boyce used a regression analysis to test their conjectures. They found that (1) the greatest change in the shift of sales from the

PITTSBURGH, PA.

City and Major Retail Centers

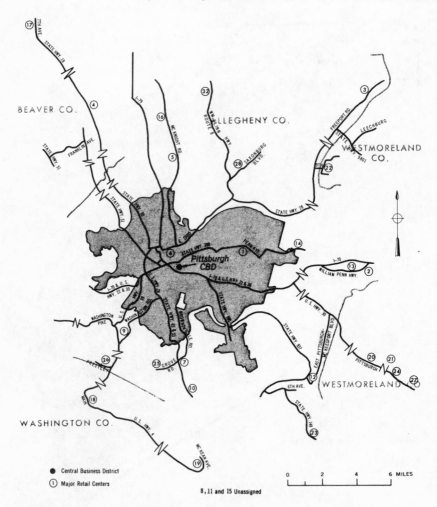

Fig. 7.2. Map page for Pittsburgh, Pa., in Major Retail Centers bulletin of the 1967 Census of Business

Census CBD to outlying areas occurs as cities approach a population of about 150,000; (2) because apparel sales remain at a constant percentage of total Census CBD sales through a large range of city sizes, they are excellent indicators of total retail sales significance in any given aggregation of business; (3) cities with substantially more Census CBD retail sales than expected are generally medium-sized cities of considerable central-place importance; and (4) cities with lower Census CBD retail sales than expected are not usually found in the "retail shadow" of a larger city, but rather are closely associated with industrially depressed areas.

A SPECIALIZATION INDEX FOR COMPARING CENSUS CBDS

Robert Reynolds manipulated the percentages of sales found in each Census CBD retail group and, by relating individual Census CBD group percentages to national percentages, derived a specialization index for comparing the CBDs.[2] For 90 cities, he used Census CBD retail sales from the 1954 Census of Business. A wide range of retail specialization was found among the Census CBDs as well as diverse directions, although general merchandise or apparel-accessory stores or both appeared as a direction of specialization in every city studied. A decided tendency for the larger-city Census CBDs to be more specialized than the smaller-city ones was noted.

Reynolds derived "cofficients of specialization" and "specialty quotients." He said that sales volume should give a more accurate picture of retail specialization than the employment data commonly used for such calculations. In any event, the latter are not published for Census CBDs. That the larger cities should be more specialized in their Census CBD sales than the smaller cities is to be expected, Reynolds pointed out, because smaller cities often have sales by food stores and automobile dealers in their Census CBDs whereas in larger cities these sales more often are made in neighborhood shopping centers and "automobile rows." But the correlation between specialization and size is far from perfect. For example, Allentown, one of the smaller cities of the 90 studied, ranked first in CBD retail specialization but it was closely followed by Dallas and St. Louis, much larger cities; and close to the other end of the scale Louisville and Boston stood out as large cities whose Census CBDs were not very specialized.

SPATIAL VARIABLES AND CBD SALES

In a study published in 1963, Ronald Boyce and W. A. V. Clark began by pointing out the significance of Census CBD retail sales as the best indicator of central city viability.[3] Aside from general trends, they said, very little is known as to why Census CBDs of metropolitan areas of the same population size often differ widely in their amounts of sales. "Explanations" for such differences, they said, are plentiful. Traffic congestion,

2. Robert B. Reynolds, "Retail Specialization of Central Business Districts," *Journal of American Institute of Planners* 26, no. 4 (November 1960): 313–316.
3. Ronald R. Boyce and W. A. V. Clark, "Selected Spatial Variables and Central District Sales," *Proceedings of the Regional Science Association* 11 (1963): 167–193.

blight and obsolescence, and declining importance of mass transportation have often been considered as prime factors in the situation. These may result from differing morphological and functional characteristics of metropolises.

But few formal analyses, none using several variables, had been made of the many factors affecting the amount of Census CBD sales. Boyce and Clark attempted to relate both the amount and the percentage of standard metropolitan area sales in the CBD to five basic variables: (1) metropolitan size, (2) Census CBD centrality within the metropolis, (3) shape, or configuration of the built-up metropolitan area, (4) the amount of planned shopping center development, and (5) the amount of Census CBD office space. Of course, there are many other variables that could have been included, but the purpose of the research was to determine how much the five morphological and spatial variables listed affect the amount of Census CBD sales. Multiple regression analyses were carried out to test the relationship in each case.

THE CBD RETAIL SALES MIX, 1948–1958

The fourth study summarized here to illustrate research based on Census CBDs is by Lorne Russwurm.[4] Considerable analytical information, he said, was available for the aggregated total sales of the ten retail groups reported by the Census of Business for the Census CBD. This "retail sales mix" consists of the following ten groups: (1) lumber, building materials, hardware, farm equipment dealers; (2) general merchandise group stores; (3) food stores; (4) automotive dealers; (5) gasoline service stations; (6) apparel, accessory stores; (7) furniture, home furnishings, equipment stores; (8) eating, drinking places; (9) drug stores, proprietary stores; (10) other retail stores. But for this retail mix and its composition over time, Russwurm said, very little information is available.

His paper, he said, filled in some of the needed information, thus supplementing the work of Horwood, Boyce, Clark, and Reynolds. First, the ten retail groups are evaluated for Census CBDs in relation to standard metropolitan area population for 1958. Russwurm re-emphasized a point made earlier by Horwood and Boyce that a few of these groups appear to be particularly significant: general merchandise, apparel, furniture, and eating-drinking. He designated the four as the GAFE group and analyzed them in considerable detail for 1958. If the GAFE retail group is accepted as containing the most "significant mixture" of CBD retail sales components, then the use of these GAFE sales will provide a truly comparable measure of the retail sales position of the individual CBD. Investigating the 1948-1958 changes within the group, Russwurm stressed two facets: the varying proportions of total GAFE retail sales accounted for by individual

4. Lorne H. Russwurm, "The Central Business District Retail Sales Mix, 1948–1958," *Annals of the Association of American Geographers* 54 (1964): 524–536.

components and the relationship between standard metropolitan area population and the individual components of the GAFE groups. Simple linear regression was used and the dynamic aspects of this type of research were stressed.

Directions of the Research

Of course the four studies described by no means exhaust the possibilities, but they show the major directions of research based upon Census CBDs. It has dealt with what is often called the retail sales mix and has been based on statistical procedures.

The following are some of the questions that they have sought to answer: (1) Is the total retail business of a certain Census CBD increasing and if so at what rate? (2) What proportion of the retail sales of a standard metropolitan statistical area comes from the Census CBD? (3) What proportion of the retail sales of the city comes from the Census CBD? (4) How are these proportions changing? (5) How do they vary with the size of the standard metropolitan statistical area? (6) With population of the urbanized area? (7) How does the retail mix of the Census CBD vary with standard metropolitan statistical area population? (8) With city population?

Evaluation of the Census CBD Concept

In Chapter 3, the Murphy and Vance CBD concept was evaluated. The same sort of analysis may appropriately be applied to the CBD concept developed by the Bureau of the Census.

The Census CBD is a convenient unit for limited purposes. Primarily, it provides a basis for comparing changes in business activity in the CBD with those in the remainder of the metropolitan area of the central city and with those of past periods. This purpose seems to have been achieved. But the Census CBD is, nevertheless, a limited concept with limited possibilities.

The Census CBD is, in the first place, subjectively outlined. The local Census Tract Committee, augmented by various local additions to the committee, decides which tracts to include. Hence, the Census CBD is more of an expression of local opinion than the result of the application of any reasonably objective method of delimitation.

Nor do Census tracts appear to be rational areas for approximating central business districts. They were established originally as units larger than enumeration districts for recording the populations of urban areas. The emphasis in the case of a central business district is supposed to be almost entirely on retail business and associated services, but by definition, you will recall, each census tract is supposed to have a substantial resident population, ideally about 4,000. To achieve this end, most tracts include some blocks that are almost entirely residential. With the land-use

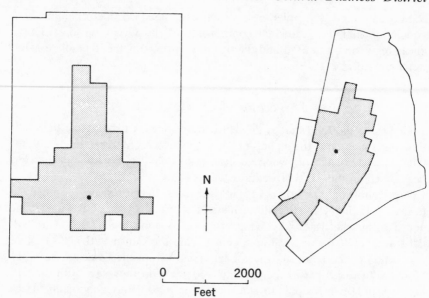

N
↑

0   2000
Feet

Fig. 7.3. Census CBDs of Phoenix, Ariz. (left), and Worcester, Mass. (right)

approach of the CBI technique such blocks would not qualify and hence would be omitted from the CBD.

This difference in approach may explain why the Murphy and Vance CBD tends to be smaller than the corresponding Census CBD (Fig. 7.3) and to have a smaller resident population. Census CBDs ordinarily are substantially larger than the central business districts outlined according to the CBI method. Here the Census CBDs of Phoenix, Arizona, and Worcester, Massachusetts, are contrasted with the districts resulting for these cities when the CBI method was used in the 1950s. The latter are shaded on the chart, with the dot in each case representing the PLVI. The outer boundary in each case is that of the Census CBD. Both cities have one-tract Census CBDs as do more than half of the cities with Census CBDs in the United States. Calculations made by the author from Census of Housing city block data show that the Worcester Census CBD has a resident population more than three times as great as that of the Worcester CBD delimited according to the CBI method and that the difference is even greater between the two Phoenix CBDs. It may be the lack of residential blocks that accounts for some critics referring to the Murphy and Vance technique as "the hard-core method."[5] In summary, the tract unit is simply too coarse for a really definitive CBD delimitation.

5. See, for example, Shirley F. Weiss, *The Central Business District in Transition,* Research Paper no. 1, City and Regional Planning Studies (Chapel Hill: Department of City and Regional Planning, University of North Carolina, 1957), pp. 17–19; and Edgar M. Horwood and Ronald R. Boyce, *Studies of the Central Business District and Urban Freeway Development* (Seattle: University of Washington Press, 1959), pp. 6–8.

In use, the Census CBD is found to have several obvious limitations. Since area was not a factor in delimiting the Census CBD, the units cannot be compared on the basis of area or in terms of data per unit of area. Referring to one of the Census CBDs, one might speak of the amount of business, or of increase or decrease in business, as a ratio to standard metropolitan statistical area population or to city population or to urbanized area population but never to Census CBD area. This characteristic is reflected in a lack of areal or geographic quality that seems to characterize much of the research based on Census CBDs. It is significant that no maps were used in any of the four research papers summarized in this chapter.

Moreover, the Census CBD is an amorphous unit. The business data for which it was designed are available for the Census CBD as a whole but not for individual blocks within it. Thus no inner differentiation of the Census CBD is possible.

The Census Bureau has made it clear that use of tracts means there is some land "not properly within a strictly defined" central business district included in a particular Census CBD, and that some small portions of a district so defined may be excluded. Their reaction, however, is that such variations do not alter significantly the magnitudes which the Census CBDs were designed to measure. By far the greater part of the city's central business, they say, is included; the amount left out is only a small fraction of the total business of the downtown area. Where empty areas or residential areas are included, it does not matter since the concern is only with absolute business totals. Defenders of the tract units for Census CBDs point out, too, the relative permanence of census tracts and also that many other data are now available by census tracts.

The Census Bureau's CBDs have their good and bad points which need to be understood by potential users. The Census Bureau did not have time or funds to go into a serious field program of CBD delimitation. The unit area they chose may represent a convenient solution but can hardly be regarded as the result of a scientific attempt to delimit the district. The tract idea was undoubtedly a simple way out and is probably adequate for its purpose. But the Bureau's adoption of a tract or several tracts as the central business district has given a certain sanction to the designated area so that people are likely to refer to it as *the* central business district. This sanction is unfortunate. To have separate business statistics for one or more central census tracts of the city is helpful. Nevertheless, the central business district concept of the Census Bureau gives no basis for comparing the central business districts of various cities as morphologic units and arriving at sound generalizations.

8

External Relationships of the CBD

This chapter continues the story of the CBD from a slightly different angle. The CBI method of delimitation held the center of the stage in Chapters 3–6, and in Chapter 7 the Census Bureau's CBD concept was discussed. It would be desirable if such tools could be used throughout the entire book but unfortunately they cannot. Many studies of the downtown, though interesting in method and content, involve no exact method of outlining a CBD. Nevertheless, they are based on the center of the city, and hence they contribute to our knowledge of the CBD and are relevant to the CBD inquiry.

The present chapter deals mostly with the external relationships of downtown. Edgar H. Horwood and Ronald R. Boyce's core-frame concept is presented; then a discussion of a possible method for outlining the CBD frame, and a study of the zone bordering the CBD; and, finally, there is a summary of some research in which opinion sampling was used in a comparison of downtown and suburban shopping in the city of Columbus.

The Core-Frame Concept

About five years after Murphy and Vance's "Delimiting the CBD" was published, Horwood and Boyce described their CBD core-frame concept.[1] Most of the studies discussed in this book involve techniques and methods which are considered worth summarizing since it is believed that knowledge of methods that have been used in CBD inquiries may well stimulate additional research. But Horwood and Boyce's work on the core-frame concept includes little by way of technique, and so does not lend itself to

1. Edgar M. Horwood and Ronald R. Boyce, "The CBD Core-Frame Concept," Chapter 2 in their *Studies of the Central Business District and Urban Freeway Development* (Seattle: University of Washington Press, 1959).

methodologic summarization. Instead, this section will consist of an analysis of the concept and its properties.

The fact that there is in the commercial heart of each city a concentrated area with a substantial vertical dimension has long been recognized. In its most pronounced form it is a relatively recent phenomenon that may be credited to the development of construction and transportation technology making many-storied buildings possible. Moreover, zoning restrictions in some cities delayed such developments until recently. Full appreciation of the vertical scale involved, however, came only with the extensive use of aerial photography. Oblique air photos of New York, Chicago, Los Angeles, Philadelphia, St. Louis, and various other cities now show these upward projecting central sections prominently.

The concentrated area that is so impressive in the downtown scene is at best only a rough approximation of the CBD, however. As pointed out in Chapter 3, there are establishments in the cluster that could hardly be considered as devoted to "central business" in any sense of the term. Even more important, there is ordinarily a bordering belt of lower buildings that also qualifies as CBD according to the CBI method of delimitation.

Let us consider further the centermost area that tends to project above its surroundings. Although Murphy and Vance recognized that the average CBD had a core-like central portion, they did not attempt to delimit a core; but, as pointed out in Chapter 2, Proudfoot, on the basis of block-frontage-volume-of-sales, had set off a CBD for Philadelphia and separated this in turn into an outer zone and an inner zone, the latter with something of the aspects of a core; Downe delimited a "hard core" for Worcester, Massachusetts, on the basis of front-foot land values; and D. H. Davies, working on Cape Town's CBD, developed a land-use method for differentiating a "hard core" (Chapter 5).

In their core-frame concept of the CBD (Fig. 8.1), Horwood and Boyce recognize the highly concentrated central area of the downtown as the "core" and refer to its bordering area as the "frame." They discuss the two areas in terms of activities present but give no rules for outlining the areas on a map.

The CBD core, as Horwood and Boyce define it, is probably the central part of the CBD of Murphy and Vance. Horwood and Boyce list a number of the core's "general properties." Intensiveness of land use is the most striking characteristic. The core stands out as having the greatest concentration of social and economic activities within the metropolitan complex. This is reflected in multistoried buildings; in high retail productivity per unit of ground area; and in land use characterized by offices, retail sales, consumer services, hotels, theaters, and banks. The core averages the highest buildings within the metropolitan complex. Linkages of personnel, they say, are largely by elevator; growth is upward through the construction of taller buildings rather than horizontal. The horizontal movement of people

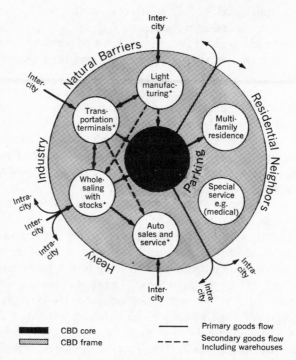

CBD core   ——— Primary goods flow
CBD frame   ----- Secondary goods flow
                                  Including warehouses

Note: The functional nodes may be concentrated in a single area, diffused in several clusters, or partially dispersed.

Source: Edgar M. Horwood and Ronald R. Boyce, *Studies of the Central Business District and Urban Freeway Development* (Seattle: University of Washington Press, 1959), Fig. 2–6.

Fig. 8.1. Graphic representation of Horwood and Boyce's CBD core-frame differentiation with selected functional centers and principle goods flows

and goods is minor, and changes in land use are likely to be limited to a few blocks over long periods of time.

The core is the area with the greatest concentration of daytime population, and there is a general absence of permanent residential population. Here is located the major mass transit interchange for the city. It is a center of specialized functions, a focus of headquarters offices for business, government, and industry. Extensive use is made of office space for executive and policy making functions. The area is a center of specialized professional and business services. Excluding natural barriers the boundaries are fixed on a pedestrian scale of distance.

There are some added restrictions on the core that are worth mentioning. For instance, Horwood and Boyce introduce the principle of a productivity standard for retail sales, with a minimum value for inclusion of an area in the CBD core. It might be expressed in retail sales per square foot. This excludes from the core considerable portions of "areas of discard" as well as off-street parking. On the other hand, space for government office use is included, since Horwood and Boyce consider such space endemic to the functioning of the CBD core.

The definition of the core, they say, does not preclude the existence of internal functional subcores. These may be centers of government, finance, style, theater, etc. Thus there may be retail and financial sectors, as in the Detroit core; and a financial subcore such as New York's which is completely separated from the retail, amusement, and office areas. These sectors are examples of the attractions of multiple nuclei.

Horwood and Boyce point out that it is at the boundaries of these CBD core subfoci that unique or ungrouped activities tend to develop. These may occur in such forms as telephone exchange buildings, court houses, libraries, or such anachronous structures as churches or fraternal establishments surviving from an earlier period. All of the foregoing are likely to have limited linkages to other CBD core activities. Frequently, they are the cause rather than the effect of subregional boundaries.

The "frame," as conceived by Horwood and Boyce, is essentially Burgess' "zone in transition." He recognized it as an area that, despite high land values based on a nearly central location, was characterized by deteriorated buildings that were technologically obsolescent as well as old. He assumed that the CBD core would expand into this transitional zone. As a matter of fact, however, such lateral growth of the CBD has been limited. Nodal development has been more characteristic of this perimetrical belt that Horwood and Boyce call the frame, the nodes taking the form of light manufacturing, wholesaling, transportation, etc. It "is not so much that activities in the core and frame are distinct from each other," they say, "but rather that different functional, geographical, and historical attributes are ascribed to the core and frame, respectively." (p. 19)

They go on to point out that the CBD frame is a uniform area readily distinguishable from all other parts of the city. In summarizing its general properties, as given by Horwood and Boyce, we may well begin with the fact that, in contrast to what was described for the core, land use is only semi-intensive in the frame. In other words, it is the area of most intensive nonretail land use. Building heights are geared to a walk-up scale. The site is only partially built upon.

The frame is an area of prominent functional subregions or nodes of land utilization (See Fig. 8.1). Subfoci are characterized mainly by wholesaling with stocks, warehousing, off-street parking, automobile sales and services, multifamily dwellings, intercity transportation terminals and facilities, light manufacturing, and some institutional uses. Unlike the core, the frame has an extended horizontal scale, geared to the accomodation of motor vehicles and goods handling. Movements between establishments are vehicular and most of the establishments have off-street parking and docking facilities. In a sense, the functional subregions are unlinked. The activity nodes are linked to transportational terminals but otherwise chiefly to areas outside the CBD frame. Establishments have important linkages to the CBD core through transportation terminals and warehouses and to out-lying urban regions. The boundaries of the frame are externally conditioned in that they are affected by natural barriers and the presence of such large homogeneous areas as residential localities with schools, shopping, and com-munity facilities. Commercial uses are generally limited to flat land. Growth extends into areas of dilapidated housing. The frame tends to fill in inter-stices of highway and rail transportation routes.

The authors point out that there is a considerable difference in the characteristics ascribed to the CBD core and the CBD frame. Within the core-frame concept the core and frame are distinct and independent func-tional units. They are two distinct regions, though the core is the more clearly defined of the two. Together the two regions constitute the CBD according to Horwood and Boyce.

The value of the core-frame concept, they say, depends to a large extent upon the purposes at hand. "However, from the standpoint of studying traffic and goods movement, central congestion, functional arrangement of establishments, business linkages, and space allocation for urban planning and redevelopment, it has been found to be a beneficial land use and functional model through which to understand the city better." (p. 22) Horwood and Boyce point out that, at the time of writing, the core-frame concept was not fully developed and was being subjected to further checks through field research.

It is interesting to compare the core-frame concept of the CBD with the CBD as delimited by the CBI method, insofar as such a comparison is possible. Apparently, Horwood and Boyce's core is somewhat smaller than the CBD based on the CBI; their core plus frame includes all of the Murphy and Vance CBD and extends considerably beyond. But their frame does not qualify as part of the CBD on the grounds outlined in Chapter 3 of this book, that the really essential central business functions appear to be the retailing of goods and services and the performing of various office functions. To include the frame as conceived by Horwood and Boyce as part of the CBD would leave a CBD with little semblance of unity.

But an equally serious objection to the core-frame concept of the CBD is the lack of an exact method for applying the idea on the map. Such a mental construct may have value for abstract conceptualization, especially in great cities, but without a delimitation technique it is hard to see how it could be used to compare CBDs and thus to arrive at generalizations.

Frame Delimitation

Although Horwood and Boyce did not give any exact rules for outlining the core or the frame on a map, a procedure for delimiting the frame of the CBD has been suggested by D. Hywel Davies for Cape Town.[2] Though it is unlikely that the rules in exactly the form used for Cape Town would be applicable to an American city, they may at least suggest the rudiments of a system that could be developed for the purpose.

The frame as delimited for Cape Town immediately surrounds the CBD and is considered to consist of "mixed goods-handling and administrative activities, of public open ground and slum housing." Surrounding the frame, except on the seaward side, lies an "inner residential zone." Although the distribution of none of the major use-categories is peculiar to the frame, five of them—automobile sales, public and government, industrial, wholesale, and commercial storage—are geographically centered in the frame so they are considered key categories for its delimitation. To these five categories it was decided to add general offices. Although centered in the CBD they are also numerous in some sections of the frame. Of the six, public and government uses were considered to form a special category, heavily concentrated in some sections of the frame near the CBD boundary. The other five are interspersed in other sections of the frame. Organizational uses, though well represented, are not considered as particularly associated with the zone and consequently are not used in delimitation of the frame.

The rules that were suggested for delimiting the CBD frame are listed here in essentially the form used by Davies for Cape Town:

1. For inclusion in the frame, a block must include at least one of these categories: automobile sales, industrial, wholesale, commercial storage, and general offices. These must occupy in total at least 5 per cent of the floor space of the block.

2. Blocks that do not qualify for the frame under Rule 1 are considered to fall within the inner residential zone if at least 20 per cent of their floor space is used for residential purposes and associated uses such as schools, corner stores, and personal service establishments. Vacant dwellings are also counted as residential.

3. Some blocks have less than 20 per cent of their floor space in residential use and less than 5 per cent in the uses listed under Rule 1 and hence fail to qualify for either the residential zone or the frame. In practice such blocks are virtually limited to public and government and organizational establishments. As such they are legitimately included in the frame.

2. D. Hywel Davies, *Land Use in Central Cape Town: A Study in Urban Geography* (London: Longmans, 1965), pp. 27–28.

4. In order to produce a simple and continuous boundary line, both inliers and outliers are ignored in the delimitation. Where a block is attached to the frame by one corner it is excluded.

When these rules were applied in Port Elizabeth it became evident that a fifth rule was needed that might read as follows:[3]

5. A block containing only industrial land use, irrespective of whether such a block also contains vacant space, and being contiguous to blocks falling within an industrial zone, shall be considered to fall within the latter zone and be placed on the outside of the line delimiting the frame.

Zone Bordering the CBD

At the heart of the American CBD it probably would be clear even to a casual observer that central business space uses dominate the scene; but with distance toward the city's edge, the proportion of central business uses declines. There are ribbons of retail development along certain radial streets, and there are outlying business areas where central-business-type uses prevail, but a general over-all outward decline continues in the proportion of such business uses. Probably the chief tendency is for a lessening of the degree of mixing of uses. Eventually come more extensive factory areas; more large residential areas; and possibly substantial physical barriers. These large use-units are interspersed, of course, with some business areas.

Somewhere with this distance outward from the city center one reaches the outer edge of the CBD. Murphy and Vance attempted to fix the boundary through certain land-use indexes. Horwood and Boyce approached the problem on a conceptual basis: somewhere, according to them, the CBD core, which had certain properties that they enumerated, gave way to the CBD frame which had somewhat different properties. But they attempted no quantitative definitions, so the two concepts cannot be areally identified for any specific locality.

Here are a few boundaries, the relative positions of which might be considered at this point: (1) The boundary of the CBD according to the CBI delimitation technique. (2) The outer edge of the CBD core according to Horwood and Boyce. They have given no precise rules for locating this boundary, but it must be nearer the city center than the Murphy and Vance CBD boundary since Horwood and Boyce omit from their core off-street parking and areas that do not reach what they consider a sufficiently high retail sales value per square foot. Commercial and customer parking areas are included in the Murphy and Vance CBD and no attempt is

3. K. S. L. Beavon, *Land Use Patterns in Port Elizabeth: A Geographical Analysis in the Environs of Main Street* (Cape Town, South Africa: A. A. Balkema, 1970), p. 17.

made to apply a productivity standard for retail trade. (3) The outer edge of Horwood and Boyce's CBD frame. The exact position of this boundary is not clear, but obviously it tends to lie a considerable distance beyond the CBD boundary based on the CBI delimitation technique.

The zone or belt just outside the Murphy and Vance CBD is of special interest because of its reputation as a problem area. It is an area of uncertainty, not enjoying the normal demand advantages of being a part of the CBD but frequently with property valuations that require high returns. Richard Preston studied this border zone which he called the "transition zone" after Burgess' usage.[4] In later phases of the work he was joined by Donald Griffin. The study was based on field mapping in three cities: Richmond, Virginia; Worcester, Massachusetts; and Youngstown, Ohio.

Table 8.1.   General types of land occupance classified as transition zone or non-transition zone in character

Transition Zone	Non-Transition Zone
Public	Areas that constitute physical barriers
Organizational	Permanent residences (including rooming houses
Wholesale	and apartment houses)
Storage	Large public open spaces
Transportational	Railroad yards
Light industrial*	Heavy industry*
Retail	Vacant lots
Service trades	Vacant buildings
Financial	
Office uses	

*Separation of all industry into light or heavy based on Harland Bartholomew, *Land Uses in American Cities,* Cambridge, Mass., 1955, pp. 147–157.
Source: Richard E. Preston, "The Zone in Transition: A Study of Urban Land Use Patterns," *Economic Geography* 42 (1966).

For each of the three cities, land use by city blocks was mapped. Field mapping and calculations from the resulting data made it possible to locate the CBD boundary according to the CBI method. With a slightly altered technique, the land use of an additional area was mapped, an area large enough to include the maximum conceivable width of the urban belt bordering but beyond the CBD boundary.

For delimiting the transition zone, Preston considered the land uses in two groups (Table 8.1). For each block he calculated the proportion of total floor space devoted to transition zone land uses and the proportion in what he considered non-transition zone land uses. Through the use of frequency graphs, he decided upon 30 per cent as the value to be used for

4. Richard E. Preston, "The Zone in Transition: A Study of Urban Land Use Patterns," *Economic Geography* 42 (1966): 236–260.

marking the outer limit of the zone in transition. For inclusion in this zone, a block had to have at least 30 per cent of its floor space in transition zone uses and be one of a contiguous group extending outward from the CBD boundary. (This amounts to a second method of frame delimitation. Compare with Davies' method.)

Preston's several end products may be briefly described. A map is given, showing for each of the three cities the extent of its transition zone; and, on a series of maps, the specific locations of various land uses within the transition zone are shown for each of the three cities. By means of a graph and a table, the relative proportions of the various specific land uses in all the transition zones combined and hence in the average transition zone for the three cities is made available.

In a later paper, Griffin and Preston summarize their ideas regarding the transition zone.[5] It is, according to them, a discontinuous belt which serves to separate the retail-oriented heart of a city from surrounding more homogeneous areas where retailing plays a less important roll. They suggest that the zone consists of sectors of "active assimilation," "passive assimilation," and "general inactivity," and show more specific use types that bear this out.

Critics have raised several questions regarding Preston and Griffin's "transition zone." Does a "unique" transition zone in fact exist? The entire city, one critic points out, is in transition; why should this particular portion of the urban area be so carefully outlined and analyzed? At another level, too, the method of delimitation of the zone is subject to question. Location of the outer boundary is based on a rather arbitrary decision as to proper transition zone uses as contrasted with non-transition zone uses.

Downtown versus Suburban Shopping: A Sampling Approach

Early in this book it was brought out that the CBD is somewhat of a problem area. One of the most serious of these problems comes about through competition with surburban shopping centers. Various studies and articles have dealt with this rivalry. But the research to be discussed here has a rather different focus. C. T. Jonassen of The Ohio State University attempted through sampling to discover the chief factors drawing people on the one hand to the CBD to procure goods and services and on the other to suburban shopping centers. His study, carried out in the early 1950s,

5. Donald W. Griffin and Richard E. Preston, "A Restatement of the 'Transition Zone' Concept," *Annals of the Association of American Geographers* 56 (1966): 339–350. For further discussion of the topic see L. S. Bourne, "Comments on the Transition Zone Concept," *The Professional Geographer* 20 (1968): 313–316, and Donald W. Griffin and Richard E. Preston, "A Reply to 'Comments on the Transition Zone Concept,'" *The Professional Geographer* 21 (1969): 232–237.

was based on Columbus, Ohio.[6] In later work, designed to check some of the Columbus findings and certain related assumptions, the earlier methods with some revision were applied to Seattle, Washington, and Houston, Texas;[7] but only the Columbus study will concern us here.

The basic idea of the work was to investigate attitudes of people living in various sections of the Columbus metropolitan area toward the use of downtown versus suburban facilities or establishments available for procuring goods and services. It sought to determine the relative importance of such factors as parking, traffic conditions, crowding, etc., in motivating different kinds of people to use one or the other place to procure goods and services. In a sense the investigation amounted to a case study, seeking through work in a single metropolitan area to shed some light on a problem of many cities: How can the CBD protect itself against competition from growing suburban shopping centers?

Throughout the bulletin in which the study was presented, the terms "downtown" and "central business district" were used synonymously to designate the central area of the city. As is often the case in such inquiries, it was not a scientifically delimited area but one which had been assumed or agreed upon locally. "In Columbus this area is bounded on the north by Chestnut Street, on the east by Fourth Street, on the south by Main Street, and on the west by Front Street." (p. 5)

The problem, Jonassen decided, resolved itself into three main components: (1) the discovery of motivating factors, (2) determination of the weights of these factors, and (3) disclosure of how they affected the decisions of different people with different characteristics to buy at a particular place.

It is hardly necessary to point out that neither the problem nor its components were simple. For example, availability of parking is an important motivating factor, but there are many related elements such as highway accessibility to areas, conditions of roads, price, and availability of a wide range of choice of goods and services in a small area. These factors may draw some people to the CBD, but others may patronize the downtown for different reasons such as the excitement, the crowds, the sociability, and the psychological stimulation of the trip. On the other hand some may deliberately avoid the downtown because these conditions distress or upset them. And it seems likely that the same factors will affect people having different value systems in different ways, and thus lead to dissimilar buying habits. People who differ in age, sex, education, occupation, socio-economic status, and place of residence may react differently to the relative attractions of the CBD and outlying shopping centers.

6. C. T. Jonassen, *Downtown Versus Suburban Shopping: Measurement of Consumer Practices and Attitudes in Columbus, Ohio* (Columbus: The Ohio State University, Bureau of Business Research, 1953).

7. C. T. Jonassen, *The Shopping Center Versus Downtown: A Motivation Research on Shopping Habits and Attitudes in Three Cities* (Columbus: The Ohio State University, Bureau of Business Research, 1955).

It was early realized that the data for the study should be obtained by interviews and that there were two possible methods of approach. The study might be based on the nature of facility, finding out how different facilities serve residents. Or the problem might be attacked from the point of view of the residents, studying how selected residents use shopping facilities and why they use those particular facilities. This would mean interviewing residents directly. Or the two possibilities might be combined. It was decided to make the study from the resident's point of view.

The first objective listed, the determination of pertinent factors, was achieved through analysis of relevant literature and through interviews. The pertinent factors were then tested in a pilot study and by field interviews and statistical analysis. Finally, a schedule of significant items was drawn up and systematically administered to a sample selected by the areal sampling technique from six selected census tracts. Various other statistical tests were derived and systematically administered. The results will be given here in general terms.

Systematic analysis of the factors associated with shopping satisfaction indicated that in Columbus the downtown had a decided advantage over suburban shopping centers. According to the analysis, the chief advantages enjoyed by the central business district were (1) a larger selection of goods, (2) the possibility of doing several errands at one time, and (3) lower prices. The most important disadvantages of the downtown were found to be (1) difficult parking, (2) crowded conditions, and (3) traffic congestion.

For the suburban shopping center the most important advantage was nearness to home, followed by easier parking and the more convenient hours kept by suburban stores. The greatest disadvantage as indicated by the study was the suburban center's lack of a large selection of goods; a second disadvantage was that not all kinds of businesses were represented there, and a third was that prices were too high.

There were various other results from the study. One, for instance, had to do with degree of inconvenience. Thus 90 per cent of the people found parking very difficult downtown. The survey indicated that the more highly educated classes, higher income groups, persons having urban or metropolitan background, and females in general indicated greater satisfaction with downtown shopping than persons of lower income, less education, rural background, and of the male sex. For the higher economic classes, a larger selection of goods was found to be more important as a downtown advantage than for people of a lower income group, and lack of a large selection in surburban centers was more of a deterrent for the upper than for the lower classes. Many other such relationships were derived, but enough have been described to illustrate the possibilities of the method.

9

Other Facets of the Downtown

In this chapter certain additional facets of the CBD are discussed. As in the preceding chapter, no exact CBD delimitation technique has been followed, but the information summarized contributes to an understanding of the city center and hence of the CBD and its problems. A brief discussion of contrasts between the CBDs of large, medium, and small cities is followed by an analysis of manufacturing in the CBD or at least in the center of the city. Then transportation in relation to the CBD is considered.

CBDs of Large, Intermediate, and Small Cities

Throughout this book we have been discussing the characteristics and problems of CBDs. In so doing we inevitably refer to city size, but only incidentally. Most of the CBDs considered were of moderate-sized cities; little attention was paid to those of very large or very small cities. The CBD has certain generally accepted qualities, specifically, a concentration of tall buildings, especially stores and office buildings; dominance of retailing and services; a concentration of people during business hours; and so on. To what extent do these characteristics occur regardless of size? Are there some that would hold good for the CBDs of New York City and Chicago, and also for the CBD of an urban center of twenty-five thousand population in an agricultural area in the Middle West?

What special characteristics are associated with the CBDs of very large cities? Normally, they have a much greater ground-floor extent than the CBDs of moderate-sized cities, with a much more pronounced vertical dimension. This latter characteristic is reflected in striking physical aspects: an observable, peaked, core area; canyon-like streets in some localities such as Wall Street in New York; and the tendency toward numerous skyscrapers.

The CBDs of very large cities seem to be more regionalized than those of smaller cities. The core contains a retail district, the most central of all central places in the geography of retailing, its stores clustered around the 100 per cent location. In or near the CBD core, there are, normally, financial and office districts, some buildings having numerous tenants but others occupied by single concerns from top to bottom. Some portions of the office area may emphasize insurance and some buildings or localities may have a reputation for specialized medical services. The CBD will have hotel clusters, one or two theater or entertainment districts, and even an area where downtown apartments are concentrated, though this is likely to be well toward the edge of the district. These various concentrations throughout the CBD are good examples of the attractions of multiple nuclei.

Undoubtedly, the tendency for internal regionalization increases with city size. Cities of 150,000–200,000 are unlikely to show very marked CBD regionalization, but in very large cities the characteristic is normal. It would be interesting to know at about what city size the change occurs and whether extent of regionalization has a predictable relationship to city population. Or is regionalization much better developed in some cities in the same size group than in others? And does this extent of regionalization vary with the type of city?

A question raised earlier in this book is whether the CBI method of CBD delimitation works with a very great city, say with a population of a million or more (see Chapter 3). We know of no case where it has been fully tried out for such a city, but there seems to be no reason other than the considerable time and effort involved why the technique could not be used. It would be interesting to apply it on a reconnaissance basis to several large cities to see how it worked out. But it would be important, in such a case, not to alter the technique in any way because of a presumed necessity to fit local conditions. Such adjustments may seem unavoidable for immediate purposes but in the process the chief advantage of the technique, comparability, will be sacrificed.

At the other extreme is the very small CBD. Can the CBI method be used to delimit the CBD in a city of 25,000? It seems doubtful. In such a small city there may only be a few, perhaps four or five, blocks that might qualify at all, and whether or not a certain block is included would be crucial, since including or excluding it might double or halve the total CB floor space. Actually, the business development in such a small place may consist only of fringes along the main street so that whole blocks seldom qualify. Also, in such small places, there may be hardly a block downtown that does not have apartments upstairs. It seems impracticable to apply the CBI technique to such an urban center. We might say that the CBD as discussed here can hardly be thought of as existing at all in a place of less than 50,000.

Manufacturing in the CBD

Manufacturing in the CBD is somewhat like resident population in the area: almost by definition there is very little of either. The Murphy and Vance CBD cannot have much factory development since blocks with factories would be likely to fall short of the required index values. Of course some largely factory blocks might be included because they were surrounded by blocks that did reach the required indexes, but this situation would be the exception; most of such enclosed blocks would have at most only minimal factory development.

The Census CBD, on the other hand, consists of one or more whole census tracts. The CBD definition furnished to local census tract committees by the Bureau of the Census makes no provision for the presence of manufacturing though it is entirely possible that, more or less by chance, a few blocks or parts of blocks in the tract or tracts selected for the CBD might be devoted to factories. But, certainly, the characterization provided by the Bureau (see Chapter 7) should mean that manufacturing land use is limited in Census CBDs.

Though neither CBD concept is likely to include much manufacturing land, we know that typically there is some industry present in the heart of the city and that various location factors are involved. One reads various descriptions of manufacturing in the downtown areas of some of our largest cities, and in these discussions the term "central business district" is common. When the term appears, however, it may be assumed that it is used only in a popular local sense to refer to a group of downtown blocks, often those between certain major streets. We have some information about manufacturing in downtown areas of New York City, but these areas are likely, ordinarily, to be somewhat larger than any scientifically defined CBDs and to contain larger resident populations.

Fortunately, Edgar M. Hoover and Raymond Vernon, in a study of the changing distribution of people and jobs in the New York Metropolitan Region, give us an account of manufacturing in New York City's "Core," which in turn includes a very limited segment on Manhattan Island mostly south of Central Park that the authors refer to as "Manhattan's Central Business District" (Fig. 9.1).[1] They say that figures on employment in the CBD are fragmentary and can only be crudely approximated, but that certain types of activity are highly concentrated there, for instance more than half of the region's "printing, publishing, and garment-making."

They comment on predominance in the area of very small establishments which must find space where it is offered for rent, that is, in buildings

1. Edgar M. Hoover and Raymond Vernon, *Anatomy of a Metropolis* (Cambridge: Harvard University Press, 1959), especially pp. 25–77.

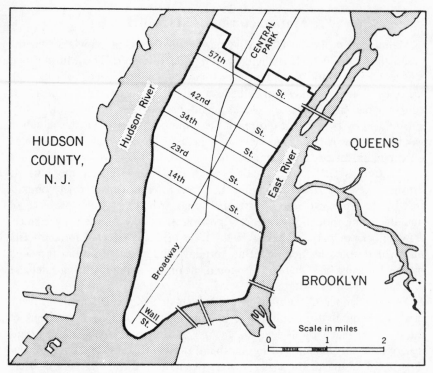

Source: Edgar M. Hoover and Raymond Vernon, *Anatomy of a Metropolis* (Cambridge, Mass.: Harvard University Press, 1959), Chart 4.

Fig. 9.1. Segment of Manhattan Island that Hoover and Vernon refer to as Manhattan's Central Business District

already in existence. The small size of establishments is reflected in the importance of "loft industries." Though this term is generally thought of as referring to clothing manufacture occupying upper stories in the downtown areas of cities, Hoover and Vernon define it for their New York City study as ". . . manufacturing space in buildings with more than one tenant, whether or not the buildings were originally designed to be multitenanted." (p. 35)

A few types of industries predominate in the New York City downtown area. Half of the loft space, according to Hoover and Vernon, is preempted by various garment and allied industries. The other half is to be found in miscellaneous loft districts available for such activities as electronics and the manufacture of chemicals and fabricated metal products. Such space can typically be had on short-term lease. Other industries associated with the downtown include the making of belts, handbags, jewelry, games, and toys; as well as business machine services and photographic services. Particularly important are printing and publishing.

Labor is an important factor in locating many downtown manufacturing units. There are some industries which typically employ unskilled labor at low wages and which are willing to accept the consequences of high turn-over and absenteeism. Most plants of this sort are likely to be in the low-priced apparel and accessory lines, in inexpensive toy production, or in the least-exacting electronics specialties. Such industries have been attracted to the Core, especially to areas where there is great crowding and hence a willingness of some to accept low-income employment. European immi-grants and, more recently, Blacks from the South and Puerto Ricans have focused on such areas.

Hoover and Vernon go on to consider external economies in the loca-tion of these small establishments. Often, for instance, a firm locates and stays in a crowded area in order to share in some essential product or service, "external" to itself. And within any given industry the smaller establishments tend to be pulled toward the crowded areas much more strongly for this reason than are their larger competitors. The small concern, moreover, may not be able, alone, to take on certain costs such as the salary of a full-time electrician, the purchase and operation of a delivery truck, or the original price and maintenance of a heavy-duty lathe. Many small plants meet these needs by subcontracting part of their work.

Small plants must be able to meet sharp increases and decreases in demand for their products. They do this partly by locating where sudden demands can be met from sources outside the plant. In this way they avoid expensive stockpiling of their materials. They have tended to stick together near the center of the urban cluster where they can get materials on short notice and quickly recruit workers for brief periods of employment, and have chosen loft space, short-run in commitment and flexible in size. Thus, Hoover and Vernon point out, the denser areas of the urban region act as a common pool for space, materials, labor, and markets.

The authors discuss at some length the role of the "communication-oriented" manufacturing industries in the New York Metropolitan Region, probably mostly in and near the CBD. There are about two dozen of these industries that stand out for possessing common traits. Each is heavily con-centrated near the center of the region and dominated by comparatively small plants. Each is an industry which needs speedy communication and transportation because of unpredictability with regard to the markets for its final products.

Industries of this sort are mainly concentrated in two groups. One consists of segments of industries producing women's underwear and related trimmings, the other of certain branches of printing and publishing. Certain other industries, such as models and patterns, signs and advertising displays, and games and toys, are included. The plants tend to be concen-trated especially in the CBD portion of Manhattan.

Speed, small size, and uncertainty of outlook are involved in the heavy clustering of these communication-oriented industries. Timeliness is very important. For instance, the printer of legal briefs or financial prospectuses sells not just the work he does but the product-by-a-certain-time. The products require consultation between customer and manufacturer.

This need for consultation and the immediacy factor account for the central location of certain types of publishing. These publishers need frequent conferences with authors, artists, and reproduction specialists. The specifications of these products and the current demands of the market cannot ordinarily be anticipated, since for the most part they are unstandardized. Another example is high-style apparel. Not only is the final product unstandardized but this is true also of the fabrics, designs, and colors that go into the final product.

The time factor is important, too, in the marketing stage. Buyers must see a great deal in as short a period as possible. In certain branches of the women's and children's apparel industry the tendency to cluster is so pronounced that most of their activity is found in one group of loft buildings in an area of 96 acres. The demand for space in the heart of the Garment Center (34th to 40th Street south of Times Square) is so great that the rental rate runs about 50 per cent higher than for similar space in other parts of the Metropolitan Region.

Hoover and Vernon point out further that, though small firms in any industry tend to cluster, the communication-oriented firms of the downtown exhibit this tendency particularly, since they depend on subcontractors for many of their auxiliary needs. Since the subcontractors furnish many diverse firms, their gross business is stable enough that they are in a better position to mechanize for specialization than are their customers. In the women's apparel industry, for example, when one group of customers ceases using a certain lining or a binding or a tape, some other group of customers may be demanding it. Thus interrelations link product uncertainty with small manufacturing establishments and these in turn with a central city location.

Of course, the manufacturing picture described is a mobile one. In the region as a whole, manufacturing is declining in the oldest city centers and Manhattan has been conspicuous in this regard. Moreover, what has been said here for downtown New York City can be no more than a rough approximation of manufacturing in the city's CBD. The true CBD is certainly much more concentrated, more limited in extent than the total of various areas of manufacturing Hoover and Vernon refer to. But the most common types of CBD manufacturing are no doubt those mentioned, and the characteristics and problems discussed are probably fairly representative of conditions in the city's CBD.

We can only assume that the types and locations of establishments the authors describe for downtown New York prevail in a general way in the CBDs of other great cities. Chicago, for example, is commonly described as having thousands of garment workers in the Loop, which is considered to approximate the city's CBD. In many cases, clothing manufacturers occupy the upper stories; in Chicago the term "loft industries" is applied particularly to these clothing factories. And the establishments are characterized by crowded conditions, small size, cheap labor, and interdependence as in the case of New York. Certainly, printing and publishing, and, no doubt, many of the other manufacturing types mentioned for downtown New York are also present in the Loop for much the same reasons.

To what extent do the CBDs of other great cities tend to have the same types of manufacturing as those described for downtown New York? And one wonders about what proportion of CBD floor space manufacturing typically occupies. Data from the nine-CBD study suggest that in cities of 200,000–300,000 manufacturing occupies only 1 or 2 per cent of total CBD floor space. Where is the manufacturing located in these smaller-city CBDs? We can at least assume it is toward the edge of the CBD rather than near the PLVI.

Looking more broadly at manufacturing in the CBD regardless of city size, light industry, of course, is likely to be most typical. This includes the industry of great city centers, such as that already described for Manhattan, and business-related industrial activities of many CBDs. So-called nuisance industries with much smoke and dirt are particularly out of place and are likely to be excluded by zoning. A few establishments are relict industries, not yet forced out by urban renewal but subject to the pressures of space needs and lawsuits. In fact industrial development of any kind is likely to be declining and on the defensive in CBDs.

Lastly, it is suggested that better generalizations are needed about manufacturing in the CBD. For any such results, the CBDs must be outlined according to some standardized method so that they are really comparable. Unfortunately, in the nine-CBD study no record was kept of types of manufacturing encountered within the mapped areas. But some such approach is necessary in order to arrive at all objectively at generalizations about manufacturing in the CBD.

Transportation and the CBD

The high degree of centrality that characterizes the CBD has long been reflected in its relation to transportation systems. In the average city, the CBD developed around the original railroad terminal though it was drawn to the harbor in the case of a port city; in later years the CBD became the focus of the highway network that developed and, more recently, of rapid transit systems. Transportation centrality of the CBD has continued but with some interesting changes. The railroad terminal function has weakened in many cities; and though the CBD remains a focus of traffic arteries, this focus has broadened. In most cities the PLVI is no longer the major automobile traffic intersection of the city. The routes have been so arranged as to avoid this bottleneck.

A real challenge in recent decades has been how to get people to the CBD, for work or shopping or entertainment, and how to get them out again. Mass transit and, where possible, rapid transit are involved. But in most cities inward and outward waves of private automobiles must be accommodated. This is accomplished by a variety of expedients. One-way streets characterize all but the most spread-out CBDs. This is particularly true in valley cities or wherever relief has restricted directions of travel. But the space problem is reflected also in a chronic shortage of parking space and in various devices related to transportation. There are, for example, highways that border and encircle some CBDs (inner-distributor loops) with parking space either as lots or as parking garages, and buses or other devices providing for the trip into the CBD. Another adjustment to the space problem is the pedestrian mall which is likely to form the heart of the modern city's CBD. And, of course, nowadays, in the whole downtown area are the specters of pollution and smog, in many instances largely products of transportation.

Two examples of transportation research will be summarized here. One has to do with daily movements of people into and out of the CBD; the other with the effects of freeways on CBDs.

DAILY MOVEMENTS OF PEOPLE INTO CBDs

The research interest in the daily movements of people into and out of the CBD had its roots in observations of nearly half a century ago. The central portion of the city, it was pointed out, is empty only as a place of residence; it may well be crowded in the daytime. The following statement has attracted a great deal of attention: "The dot map of Manhattan appears pale in those portions of the city which, from the number of persons seen on the streets one ordinarily thinks of as most congested."[2]

This statement might be applied equally well to any CBD and to the present day rather than to some earlier date. There is a substantial movement of people into the CBD in the morning and back home at night, and city administrators and city planners have long sought some simple formula for measuring this flow and of projecting it into the future. "What," they may ask, "will be the number of people coming into our CBD each morning in 1980?"

A decade or two ago, daytime population was defined by the U. S. Bureau of the Census as follows: "For any given standard location the daytime population at the selected hour represents the sum of the number of persons physically present in the area working, attending school, shopping, conducting personal business, enroute from one place to another, or en-

2. Regional Survey of New York and its Environs, *Population, Land Values and Government* 2 (New York, N.Y., 1929): 75.

gaging in other activities away from their homes, and the number of resident persons remaining at home in the location."[3]

Several people have worked on the problem of daytime population of the downtown. Gerald W. Breese pioneered with a study in which he attempted to describe the daytime population of the Chicago CBD for a typical weekday in May, 1940, and analyzed the trends in daytime population from 1926 through 1946.[4] To construct his pattern of daytime population he used three sources of information: (1) CBD cordon counts taken by municipal agencies; (2) supplemental origin and destination surveys; and (3) operating statistics from mass transportation and public carriers for metropolitan Chicago.

In addition to a breakdown of numbers arriving in the CBD by various means of transportation, Breese analyzed accumulation patterns and hourly fluctuations, length of stay, daily and seasonal fluctuations, daytime and evening differences, and numbers entering the CBD for specific purposes. In his work, he used a simple method of analysis in reporting on specific purposes of trips: employees, permanent residents and hotel guests, and pedestrians. But Breese found it impossible to arrive at any figure for the number of shoppers in the CBD or for persons there for any reason except residence and employment. Therefore, he considered pedestrians as a sort of index of those persons who were in the area mainly for other than employment or residence. Thomas Weir, in a study of the daytime population of Winnipeg, found similar limitations: the transient and mobile groups presented the chief data difficulties.[5]

In his study of the daytime population of the Central Business District of Chicago, Breese pinpointed some interesting relationships. High off-peak flows (when employed persons were generally in their offices and shops) focused around the department stores and other commercial establishments in the areas of high land values.

Other later studies of movements of people into CBDs have found destination studies conducted by the Bureau of Public Roads useful. These have helped in determining trip purpose. And Donald Foley, working with Breese originally, developed methods of standardizing the measures of persons entering the central business district.[6]

3. U.S. Bureau of the Census, *Population Estimates for Survival Planning* 1 (Prepared for the Federal Civil Defense Administration, Department of Commerce, 1956): 9.

4. Gerald W. Breese, *The Daytime Population of the Central Business District of Chicago with Particular Reference to the Factor of Transportation* (Chicago: University of Chicago Press, 1949).

5. Thomas R. Weir, "A Survey of the Daytime Population of Winnipeg," *Queen's Quarterly,* vol. 67, no. 4 (Winter 1961) and "Land Use and Population Characteristics of Central Winnepeg," *Geographical Bulletin,* no. 9 (1956), pp. 5–21.

6. See Donald L. Foley and Gerald Breese, "The Standardization of Data Showing Population Movement into Central Business Districts," *Land Economics* 27 (1951): 348–353; and Donald L. Foley, "The Daily Movement of Population into Central

(continued on p. 132)

The various studies of movement of people into the CBD, however, have suffered from a serious limitation. In nearly all cases a CBD boundary has been arbitrarily assumed, so comparisons between cities are decidedly suspect.

FREEWAY IMPACT

A type of urban transportation research that has attracted the attention of a number of geographers as well as engineers and others interested in the city has dealt with the effects of freeways and expressways. An *expressway* is commonly defined as a divided arterial highway for through traffic with full or partial control of access, in contrast to a *freeway,* which amounts to an expressway with full control of access. What have been the measurable beneficial economic effects on urban centers of the building of such routes? Conversely, what have been the adverse economic effects on a community of being bypassed? In the present instance our focus is not the city but the CBD, so the questions asked have to do with the measurable effects of the coming of such a route to the CBD.

About a decade ago, the author with some associates undertook a study of the effects of freeways on CBDs.[7] When a freeway passes so close to the city's CBD or terminates so near this central area as to facilitate the flow of traffic to and from the CBD, we argued, it should be possible to measure its effects. Observable changes in the business activities of the district might reasonably be expected to occur.

Little previous research regarding freeway impact has focused directly upon the CBD.[8] But a study of the literature on impact studies in general suggested the following as some of the possible measures to be considered in such research: land values inferred from repeat sales data; land use, especially in strips along the highway; business activity inferred from sales tax data; traffic obtained from counts; opinions based on sampling; and changes in activity as reflected in commercial and residential building permits.

Our first problem was to focus on several comparably sized cities where the CBD was reached by a freeway which had been in existence long enough for its effects to be observable and measurable. This problem was

---

Business Districts," *American Sociological Review* 17 (October 1952): 538–543, and "Urban Daytime Population: A Field for Demographic-Ecological Analysis," *Social Forces* 33 (1954), 323–330.

7. See Robert J. Huhtanen, Paul J. Mika, Richard E. Preston, and Raymond E. Murphy, *A Study of the Effects of Freeways on Central Business Districts* (Report submitted to U.S. Department of Commerce, Bureau of Public Roads, February 1961).

8. For an exception see Edgar M. Horwood and Ronald R. Boyce, *Studies of the Central Business District and Urban Freeway Development* (Seattle: University of Washington Press, 1959). However, the title is somewhat misleading since most of the book deals with methods of studying changes in the central area of the city, and impact of freeways on CBDs is discussed only in the last chapter.

found to be extremely difficult. Those cities of reasonable size that had such freeway-CBD connections had had them for such short periods that measurable effects were hardly to be expected. The problem was further complicated by the fact that the downtown areas of some cities were undergoing such extensive urban renewal projects that realistic land-use maps were almost impossible to prepare. Nevertheless, three cities were decided upon: Richmond, Virginia; Oakland, California; and Long Beach, California.

The several measures mentioned earlier were considered, but most of them were found to be impracticable for one reason or another. They were considered to some degree, but chief dependence in our research was placed on land-use mapping. A map of current land use was constructed for the downtown area of each city and—a far more difficult task—of the same area for a period just before building of the freeway began. Then maps were made for each of the three CBDs to show the location of changes in square feet of space devoted to commercial parking, changes in square feet of space devoted to customer parking, changes in total traffic volume on major streets at the CBD boundary, contrasts in traffic by streets within the CBD, changes in Central Business Intensity Index by blocks, and changes in Central Business Height Index by blocks.

The project did not attain as substantial results as we had hoped it would, but it was of considerable interest from the viewpoint of method-ology. The chief difficulty as it turned out was the one anticipated in ad-vance, that the freeways had not been in existence long enough in any of the three cases for pronounced land-use changes to be expected.

The following tentative generalizations were suggested as a result of our work: (1) A freeway not especially designed to serve the CBD is likely to have little effect on the CBD, at least for a short-run period. (2) Free-ways always relieve congestion on other routes. (3) A new office building or other large developments that generate growth may exert a greater pull on the CBD than the freeway. (4) Tolls may prevent a freeway from hav-ing its fullest possible impact. (5) The degree to which a freeway ties in with existing street and flow patterns is an important factor in determining its impact. (6) A freeway invariably results in a reorientation of traffic in the CBD. (7) Adjustments to a freeway are more likely to take place in the zone surrounding the CBD than in the CBD itself.

Horwood and Boyce, commenting on the difficulties of studying urban freeway impact on the city center, point out a number of variables inherent in the problem which make it almost impossible to segregate highway im-pact from other factors that bring change to the CBD. These include the extent of the freeway network and the degree of its completion, character-istics of the inner-distributor loop, amount of space utilized for freeways, linkage interference by freeway splitting of land functions, the degree of centralization or decentralization of activities, the extent of planning and urban renewal, the development of mass transit, provision for off-street parking, and changes in the CBD itself which are occurring independent of highways.[9] And they very properly call attention to simultaneous changes in the urban economy that may have so much effect as largely to obscure freeway impact on the CBD. These include, they say, interregional migration, defense spending, national market conditions, the availability and adequacy of water, industrial waste problems, labor conditions, and the sheer multiplying effects of urban growth itself.

An extremely important factor in the whole matter of freeway impact on the CBD is definition. As Horwood and Boyce point out, the area they call the CBD frame is primarily dependent upon external linkages. The inner-distributor freeways will be likely to have increased value for warehousing, wholesaling, and the like, which tend to develop in the frame. So we come back to the matter of CBD definition. In the terms in which the CBD is defined in this book it is the area just outside the CBD that is likely to be most affected by the hypothetical freeway.

9. Edgar M. Horwood and Ronald R. Boyce, *Studies of the Central Business District and Urban Freeway Development* (Seattle: University of Washington Press, 1959), p. 125.

10

CBD and Suburbs in Competition

Up to this point the central business district inquiry has dealt largely with static phenomena. Little of the time element has been involved, though in a few instances action has been referred to casually as in the research work summarized under transportation, and concepts such as the zone of assimilation and zone of discard were discussed where motion was implicit. The topics and the treatment nonetheless have amounted largely to the analyses of static situations.

The time element will be brought more definitely into the present chapter in connection with two investigations. Both are concerned with the downtown and the suburbs in competition through time. The first inquiry, published in the early 1950s, consists of a case study of the degree to which the Madison, Wisconsin, Central Business Area is holding its own against suburban retail centers. The second is similarly practical in nature. It involves the degree to which administrative offices in American cities are suburbanizing as evidenced by what is going on in the San Francisco Bay Area.

Functional Change in Downtown Areas

The work on Madison, Wisconsin, was done by Richard Ratcliff in the early 1950s and was a study of functional change in what he called the Madison Central Business Area.[1] In this case study he hoped to gain information that might be of practical value to people concerned with city affairs anywhere in the country. Thus it was applied research but had an historical element, too, since it involved changes through time.

An urban phenomenon that has attracted a good deal of attention in recent decades has been peripheral retail expansion. This has taken the

1. Richard U. Ratcliff, *The Madison Central Business Area: A Case Study of Functional Change,* Wisconsin Commerce Papers, vol. 1, no. 5 (Madison: Bureau of Business Research and Service, University of Wisconsin, 1953).

form of new retail centers springing up in outer portions of cities of all sizes and huge regional shopping developments at the edges of large metropolises. These retail developments characteristically duplicate many of the central area retail facilities. In addition they are replete with parking space and are closer to the homes of the customers than are the downtown facilities.

In interpreting this phenomenon, Ratcliff says, the most commonly held hypothesis is that the peripheral retail expansion is occurring at the expense of the central area, that a literal decentralization is taking place, a dispersal of retail facilities from center to outskirts. A logical extension of this thinking is that the central retail district ultimately will decline in volume of business and in land values.

The alternative hypothesis is that the peripheral growth of retail facilities is merely in proportion to the population increase and spatial expansion of our urban areas. According to this hypothesis the central areas will continue to grow in productivity and business volume, and property values will continue to rise as the total population of the urban area increases, though perhaps at a slower rate than the population. The spectacular spurt of recent years in outlying retail development is merely a temporary acceleration of a normal growth process. But this does not mean that the central area will retain a constant or increasing proportion of the total retail business of the community. In fact there is historical evidence that, as cities grow, the central area normally accounts for a decreasing proportion of the commercial activity.

Ratcliff's research addressed itself to the problem of testing the validity of the alternative interpretations. Is dispersion or decentralization good or evil for the community? Will it destroy the central area or at least cause serious damage to property owners and to merchants? How will it affect the tax base?

Several approaches appear possible. Why not examine property values directly? The fact is, though, we have very inadequate data on central land values, since there are so few transactions of purchase or sale involving central properties within any reasonable length of time and they are particularly hard to unravel because of changing values of the dollar.

Sales volume or net profits for central or outlying retail stores by type of outlet might be useful if such data were available for a sufficient period of time. But the 1935 and 1948 Censuses of Business afforded only a limited comparison for a few large cities; they represented too short a time span and the retail types for which data were shown were not sufficiently refined.

One final line of attack remained for testing the alternative explanations of retail diffusion. This, Ratcliff called the "functional approach." Are the shifts in the pattern of retail distribution basic changes which presage a modification in the services available at the center and in the pattern of activities that has up to now characterized this focal zone? Are the changes

in retail distribution only matters of degree? Are they simply a continua-
tion of what has been happening in cities for some time? Or, finally, though
these changes may be basic, is it possible that they may nevertheless be
without serious detriment to the central area?

The technique of functional analysis starts with an examination of the
types of retail outlets represented in the central area and a classification of
these use-types. A history of the types and number of outlets covering a
sufficient period of time in a given city may show significant trends. We
might expect to find a decline in the number of representatives of certain
types of retail outlets, an increase in others; the complete disappearance
of some types and the appearance of new ones. How can these changes in
the central retail structure be interpreted so as to throw light on the future
of the central business district?

To illuminate this problem, Ratcliff undertook an historical analysis of
the Madison, Wisconsin, central area as a case study. The city had a population of 110,000 in its urbanized area in 1950 which is approximately when
the Madison study began. By recording and interpreting the growth and
changes in the number and nature of the business establishments in the
central area of Madison over a 30-year period, he hoped to be able to
choose intelligently between the two alternative hypotheses.

The research was for the purpose of determining whether or not the
changes that are taking place in the pattern of commercial uses in the city
are destructive of values in the center. First, Ratcliff undertook to describe
the changes in terms of services which characterize the central area.

The district selected for analysis is the central portion of Madison, Wisconsin (Fig. 10.1). This was divided for the analysis into Area A and Area
B. Area A is representative of the most intensive retail part of the downtown, the retail core. It includes Capitol Square, the first two blocks of
State Street, and certain other extensions. (Its extent is indicated in Figure
10.1 by a shaded border.) Area B, surrounding Area A, is open-ended in
the sense that it includes the remainder of the district shown on the map
and might as well have had its boundary drawn still farther out. It is a
broader zone of mixed residential, commercial, and public land use. In
short, the two areas were not defined on any very logical basis. Ratcliff
rarely used the term central business district throughout his case study,
but, if delimited according to the CBI method, Madison's CBD would include Area A and probably a substantial portion of Area B as well.

The historical recording of land uses and occupancies in the central area
began with 1921 and was carried through at approximately five-year intervals: 1925, 1931, 1935, 1941, 1946, and 1950. Ground-floor non-residential occupancies were recorded by street addresses, obtained from city directories of those years. One hundred fifty-four categories were used, the
number of representatives of each class for each of the seven points of
time being determined for Area A, Area B, and the two areas combined
(Table 10.1).

Table 10.1. *Method of classification of various land-use types for Area A and Area B in Madison for selected years, 1921–1950, and of recording data used by Ratcliff in his Madison Central Business Area study*

Type	Area	1921	1925	1931	1935	1941	1946	1950
Accountant	A	—	—	—	—	—	1	2
	B							1
	A+B					—	1	3
Advertising-Agency	A	—	1	1	3	2	—	3
	B							
	A+B	—	1	1	3	2		3
Agricultural Implements	A	2	1	1	1	1	1	—
	B							
	A+B	2	1	1	1	1	1	
Antiques	A	—	—	1	—	—	1	1
	B							
	A+B	—	—	1	—	—	1	1
Appliance	A	—	1	5	4	2	3	2
	B			1	3	2	5	3
	A+B	—	1	6	7	4	8	5
Architect	A	—	—	1	—	—	1	1
	B							
	A+B	—	—	1	—	—	1	1

Land-use type		C1	C2	C3	C4	C5	C6	C7
Associations, Social	A	1	2	2	2	2	2	2
	B	5	7	6	7	8	10	11
	A+B	6	9	8	9	10	12	13
Associations, Trade	A	1	—	2	—	1		1
	B					1	1	1
	A+B	1	—	2	—	1	1	2
Auto Accessory	A	1	3	1	2	1	—	1
	B		3	1				
	A+B	1	6	2	2	1	—	1
Auto Battery and Tire	A	6	2	2	2	2	2	2
	B	5	7	4				1
	A+B	11	9	6	2	2	2	3
Auto Body	A	1	—	1	1	1	—	—
	B							
	A+B	1	—	1	1	1	—	—

Note: The number of representatives of the land-use type is shown in each case. This is the first of 13 pages of similar data that appear as Appendix Table I in Ratcliff, *The Madison Central Business Area*, Madison, Wis., 1953, p. 51.

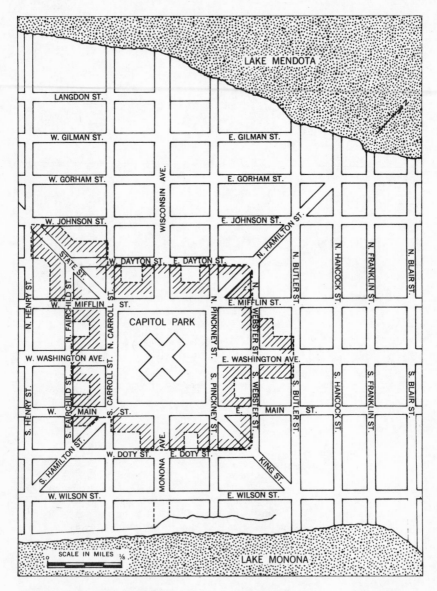

Source: Richard U. Ratcliff, *The Madison Central Business Area, A Case Study of Functional Change* (Madison: Bureau of Business Research and Service, School of Commerce, University of Wisconsin, 1953) Vol. 1, No. 5, Chart 1 with modifications.

Fig. 10.1. Central Madison, showing Area A and Area B as used in Ratcliff's study

The limitation of the coverage to ground-floor occupancies was not intended as a negation of the growing importance of upper-floor offices in central areas. The shifts in office use were significant, of course. But it was decided in this study to focus on the more intensive central land uses, particularly retail services, which were "the current concern of property owner, merchant, and tax collector."

The terms used in the city directories have not been fully descriptive and often have not been entirely consistent from year to year. Therefore, there was little combining of categories in the research; the original designations were adhered to as much as possible. At the same time it was realized that, over the years, changes in the pattern of merchandising have brought changes in the nature of goods and services offered by retail stores. Changes in drug stores are a good example and retail grocery outlets have changed even more. It was obvious that continuing to follow the original categories was not a perfect answer to this anomalous situation, but, nevertheless, it was the method followed perforce in this research.

Assembling of data made possible various lines of inquiry, the first having to do with the number and variety of outlets. The general conclusion reached was that in 1950 the variety of goods and services in the central area ground-floor locations was not significantly different from what it had been in 1925. This situation was true of Area A and of the peripheral segment, Area B, as well.

Ratcliff next examined what he referred to as minus mutations and plus mutations. By the former he meant types that gave evidence of a decline in importance with the passage of time and the growth of the Madison community (Table 10.2). Prominent among the minus mutations were some of the neighborhood-type outlets. Here, Ratcliff included grocery, hardware, meat and fish markets, drugs, liquor, and shoe repair. He discussed the coming of the supermarket and other reasons for general decline in the group and brought out contrasts between Area A and Area B. Another group of services that showed definite tendencies to decline in the central area included auto accessory, auto tire and battery, filling stations, paint and wallpaper, and sporting goods. In general the decline seems to have been due to these types moving closer to their particular clientele. The several other declining land-use groups were similarly identified and discussed, together with the reasons that seemed to account for their decline.

Among the non-residential uses which increased in importance, thus showing plus mutations, was one group composed of business services and another consisting of department store, variety, and women's clothing along with various specialty shop types—furs, gifts, children's clothing, shoes, and jewelry.

These lists are by no means complete but serve to bring out something

Table 10.2. Examples of minus mutations, number of representatives

Type	Area	1921	1925	1931	1935	1941	1946	1950
Grocery, Retail	A	8	9	10	10	6	5	4
	B	7	5	3	7	5	5	4
	A + B	15	14	13	17	11	10	8
Drugs	A	12	13	15	12	9	10	9
	B	1	2	2	1	1	1	1
	A + B	13	15	17	13	10	11	10

Source: Table 5 in Ratcliff, *The Madison Central Business Area*, Madison, Wis., 1953, p. 18.

of the methods used by Ratcliff. There were, it may be added, some land-use types that remained essentially static. Among such types in Area A were bakery (retail), florist, shoe shine and hat, threater, loan company, and bank. The other static types were found in both A and B or in Area B only.

In an "Evaluation and Conclusion" chapter Ratcliff brings together his conclusions as to whether or not the centers of cities are declining in pro-ductivity and losing in land-value levels. His findings as to changing num-bers of store-type occupancies are supplemented by data on front foot usage by principal store-type groups in Area A.

The Madison central area was found to have remained fairly constant in number of non-residential ground-floor establishments while the com-munity grew substantially in population. This situation was not, however, considered necessarily a danger signal. Ratcliff says that an adequate test of deterioration of a central area must take account of changes in land use by outlets of varying degrees of productivity or rent-paying ability. Changes in the proportion of shopping goods outlets may be taken as a final test of the direction in which the central area is moving. So long as the shopping goods outlets are holding their own, land values will also hold steady; if these types are absorbing an increasing share of central area space, the central area is prosperous.

This test was applied to the central area of Madison by summarizing data relating to land use in Area A and supplementing these "number of stores" data by "front footage" data. Both approaches showed a significant increase in proportionate land use by the shopping goods outlets (depart-ment, variety, women's clothing, men's clothing, children's clothing, shoes, furs, jewelry, gifts) during the full period of the study. And there was some replacement of less intensive land uses by the more intensive uses in the shopping goods group. Front footage data given in one of Ratcliff's tables definitely confirm this increase in the proportion of shopping goods outlets. All this clearly indicates a continuing replacement of less intensive uses with more intensive uses, of types with lower rent-paying capacity with higher rent-paying types, and of non-commercial or non-retail uses, con-venience goods outlets, and specialty goods outlets by shopping goods out-lets. This replacement should be accompanied by a steady increase in ag-gregated land values in Area A thus confirming the stability of Madison's central business district.

In terms of total accessibility the Madison central area has certain ad-vantages which are true, of course, of the average CBD. More people can get to the center more expeditiously than to any other spot in the city. Measured by total accessibility the central area is the most convenient for the greatest number of persons for the greatest variety of purposes.

It has even greater advantages over the remainder of the urban area in terms of availability. There is a greater number of different services than at any other locality in the urban area, and also the central area has the greatest number of various combinations of such services, a wider range for choice than in any other district in style, price, and quality.

If the hypothesis is correct that the prime advantages of the central area over outlying retail centers is convenience for the greatest number of consumers in terms of (1) variety of services and (2) range of choice among services, then an important indicator of central deterioration would be a loss or decline of this advantage. How has the Madison central area fared in these respects? Obviously, traffic congestion and parking difficulties reduce the advantages of the central area. Obviously, too, outlying and competing shopping centers have expanded in number and in variety of services offered. But the central area still appears to have a net total advantage of convenience in the availability of the widest variety of goods and services, especially those of shopping goods outlets. But if productivity is not to suffer, Ratcliff says, the strong tendency toward decreasing accessibility to consumers must be offset and the advantage of a wide variety of services must be protected.

He emphasizes the importance of maintaining accessibility for the central area through such positive steps as: (1) more efficient use of the street system through traffic routing and control; (2) improvements in the street system through widening and developing of throughways; (3) additional parking facilities and better parking control; and (4) spreading the load on the system by staggering beginning and quitting times and by maintaining evening shopping hours.

Urban renewal of close-in districts, he says, may help, particularly any development that will increase the daytime population of the central area. New office buildings in the downtown are a case in point. In some cities there is a tendency for large non-retail establishments employing hundreds of office workers to move to suburban areas. This can be a real threat to the downtown but can sometimes be forestalled through downtown urban renewal which provides desirable close-in space for the offices, since after all the downtown location can offer many conveniences for the employees.

It should be re-emphasized that the work on Madison is a case study. Such a study does not lead to widely applicable generalizations. As Ratcliff himself points out, the findings of one case study cannot be definitive, but there is sufficient uniformity in structure among American cities so that some of the findings may have general application.

If the Madison case is at all representative, it would appear that the cause of central areas is far from hopeless. They have a major advantage in availability of shopping goods and related lines, and their location gives them a potential advantage in accessibility. The latter is threatened by traffic and parking problems and by lack of appropriate facilities for certain types of mass employment. But the relative growth of shopping goods lines in the central area is encouraging.

Suburbanization of Administrative Offices in Metropolitan Areas

The second study to be summarized in this chapter was carried out by Donald Foley.[2] Like Ratcliff's work on Madison it was a case study and like that study, too, it is applied research and also has an historical element since it involves changes through time. Though based on the San Francisco Bay Area, it deals with a problem facing most large urban areas. Ratcliff studied the suburbanization of retailing; Foley investigated suburbanization of administrative offices and its possible effects on the downtown. Thus both were concerned with the health of CBDs or at least of the central areas of cities.

Suburbanization of residences, retail trade and services, and manufacturing, Foley says, are inevitable in view of our evolving transportation and communications. But nationwide evidence suggests that executive and regional offices, too, may be shifting to suburban sites. This raises new questions. The suburbanization of administrative offices could have serious effects indeed on downtown centers. As Ratcliff points out in the summary of his Madison study, such offices have done much to sustain CBDs against the competition of suburban shopping centers.

Several main queries are considered in Foley's study: (1) To what degree have top administrative offices in the San Francisco Bay Area been suburbanizing? (Fig. 10.2) (2) Which types of offices have shown the greatest tendency to move from the central districts? (3) What factors are taken into account in deciding whether to relocate an office? (4) What office locational trends may be expected during the coming years?

How representative of other large metropolitan areas can a case study be, based as this one is on the San Francisco Bay Area? How generally applicable can we expect the results to be? The physical development around the massive water area of the Bay makes for atypicalness, but San Francisco's historical importance as a West Coast regional center has fostered a strong downtown financial-office district similar to its counterpart in the Eastern seaboard metropolis. Business activity, population, and the physical pattern of the Bay Area are growing vigorously. The four questions raised deal with the effects of this West Coast automobile-age growth on a downtown office concentration much like those of older Eastern cities.

The main sources of information for the study were: (1) a telephone survey of approximately 1,100 San Francisco Bay Area firms or nongovernmental organizations employing over 100 persons each in 1953; (2) personal interviews with about 60 executives, consultants, and real estate

2. Donald L. Foley, *The Suburbanization of Administrative Offices in the San Francisco Bay Area,* Research Report 10, Real Estate Research Program (Berkeley: Bureau of Business and Economic Research, University of California, 1957).

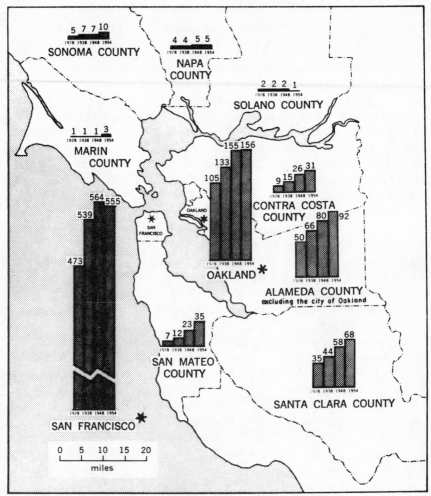

Source: Donald L. Foley, *The Suburbanization of Administrative Offices in the San Francisco Bay Area* Research Report 10, Real Estate Research Program (Berkeley: Buerau of Business and Economic Research, University of California, 1957), Fig. 7 with modifications.

Fig. 10.2. Growth of top administrative offices in the San Francisco Bay Area, 1928–1954

specialists in the Area; and (3) a review of reports on other metropolitan areas and discussions of their problems.

   Limits of the study need to be pointed out. The locational trends for government offices are not covered in the study. Only "large" firms or organizations in terms of Bay Area employment were included. Firms that typically are individually small but that collectively use important blocks of office space, such as, law offices, brokerage firms, and manufacturers' representatives, were not included. Details regarding offices, such as square-foot areas and characteristics of office space, were not studied. Tabulations dealt with "offices" and "firms" in an unweighted sense. Volume of business, size of office force, and amount of office space were not considered. Thus the need for other approaches supplementary to the one used in the present study is clear.

Throughout the study the downtown areas are referred to chiefly as "central districts" or "the central area" or "central San Francisco" or "central portions of the Bay Area." They include central San Francisco, central and northwestern Oakland, Berkeley, and Emeryville. Foley made no attempt to delimit a CBD so his study reflects CBD conditions in only a very general way.

Since the word "office" is loosely and variously used, he considered it necessary as background for his report to define certain terms. For instance, a *large firm or organization* was defined as a business or industrial firm or other nongovernmental organization with an average nine-county Bay Area employment exceeding 100 persons in 1953. (He identified 1,073.)

A *top administrative office* was a single, main Bay Area administrative office from which a firm or organization that qualified for inclusion in the study managed its Bay Area and possibly more extensive operations. (Of the 1,073 firms, 959 had top administrative offices of this sort.)

A *special administrative office* was an important administrative office (other than a top administrative office) that a qualifying firm or organization maintained to manage particular functional, product, or geographic divisions of its Bay Area operations. (There were 183 of these special administrative offices, 145 offices of firms that had no single top administrative office and 38 administrative offices maintained by firms in addition to top offices. Minor administrative offices were included when as a group they functioned as the equivalent of a single top office.)

An *office move* was the case in which at the end of one of the three periods studied (1928–1938; 1938–1948; 1948–1954) the street address of a top administrative office was more than a city block from its street address at the beginning of the period.

A *new office* was a top administrative office that was in existence at the end of a period but had not been in existence in comparable form at the beginning of that period.

A *detached office* was an administrative office not located within a city block of any relatively important non-office type of establishment—store, factory, warehouse, terminal facility—operated by its firm or organization.

An *attached office* was an administrative office located within a city block of a non-office type of establishment such as those listed for a detached office.

Foley next proceeded to a summarization of his findings. During the second quarter of the twentieth century, he said, the proportion of top administrative offices in central San Francisco dropped steadily from 61 per cent of all Bay Area top offices in 1928 to 49 per cent in 1954. At the same time the number of top offices locating in relatively distant suburban areas has shown a decided gain. Thus the proportion of offices located in sections that were at least one hour's peak-hour travel time by automobile from downtown San Francisco increased from 23 per cent of all Bay Area offices in 1928 to 37 per cent in 1954.

Suburban top offices relocated or first established in this period were almost all attached to non-office facilities such as manufacturing plants, warehouses, or transportation terminals.

In addition to establishing or relocating top offices in suburban areas, large firms are showing an increasing tendency to establish one or more offices in suburban and subcenter locations to supplement the continuing role of an office in the metropolitan center. The top office may stay downtown while certain district sales or administrative offices may be established in outer locations; or an accounting or a research office may be suburbanized; or a sales office may be left in the center and a regional administrative office moved out.

The relocation of important top detached offices to the suburbs has been negligible. Of the grand total of 725 office moves or newly established offices identified during the study only five top offices of firms surveyed were detached-status suburban offices.

The central portions of the Bay Area (central San Francisco, central and northwestern Oakland, Berkeley, and Emeryville) together have retained a striking concentration of administrative offices. About 65 per cent of all Bay Area top offices still lie within this central area and 49 per cent are clustered in central San Francisco. Figures based on a weighting for size of office would show even greater concentrations in these respective central areas.

It is of interest to examine the reasons given for locating the administrative office in a suburban area in contrast to those favoring locating in the central district of the metropolitan area. These reasons were so varied, Foley points out, that any single weighted configuration with broad applicability was out of the question.

The reasons stressed for locating the administrative office in a suburban area were: (1) to be associated with a manufacturing plant or other operating facility which is considered to be advantageously located in a suburban district; (2) to permit employees to live in the suburb with a short trip to work; (3) to gain flexible and expandable office space with the amenities that go with a suburban location; (4) to attract and hold workers at relatively low wages; (5) to reduce office rental cost; (6) to escape from downtown congestion; (7) to locate near the establishments of other firms to which ease of access is considered advantageous.

Reasons given for locating the administrative office in a central district of the metropolitan area included: (1) to maintain ease of access to the central district and to the metropolitan area as a whole; (2) to take advantage of first-class office space which is available in the central core; (3) to stay within easy reach of the office worker labor market; (4) to be easily accessible to business and professional services and other external economies of the central portions of the Bay Area; (5) to locate with an operating establishment such as department store or newspaper that needs the locational advantage of a central district; (6) to maintain a traditional location and one that has prestige; (7) to be readily available to the out-of-town visitor.

Of course many other, slightly less definite influences, may come to bear on any specific decision. Detached offices obviously have a far greater choice of location, but most top administrative offices are attached to operating establishments whose locational needs may be the ruling consideration. Another interesting factor is the attitude of the community under consideration. Some communities in the Bay Area promote the development of special administrative offices; others, perhaps more completely residential in character, discourage them.

More detailed findings regarding office suburbanization between 1928 and 1954 are presented in Chapter II of Foley's report, together with illustrative maps, graphs, and tables. The present geographic distribution of Bay Area administrative offices is described in Chapter III, and office location from the firm's viewpoint is considered in Chapter IV. But these three chapters are not discussed here since they amount to elaborations and supporting evidence for the findings already covered in the summary of Foley's work.

In a final chapter of his report Foley advances some conjectures as to future office location in the area, and discusses needed further research, together with data-gathering problems involved.

11

The Changing CBD

In the studies of Madison and of the San Francisco Bay area an investigation of changes through time constituted the central theme. In this chapter the several inquiries focus even more definitely upon the temporal factor. First, the changing outline of the Harrisburg CBD is traced through three-quarters of a century. A second, more subjective study follows in which the emergence of Boston's CBD over a period of more than a century and a half is considered. A third discussion deals with a study of location changes in the core of Philadelphia. The chapter concludes with a summary of methods used in the studies of CBD change.

Outlining the CBD for Past Periods: the Harrisburg Case

Interest in the CBD is by no means restricted to the district of today. It may be particularly rewarding to consider its extent at various times in the past as well. But how can we delimit the CBD for a much earlier period or for a succession of such earlier periods? It is one thing to make a current urban land-use map as a basis for delimiting the CBD but quite another to reconstruct land-use patterns of the past for this purpose.

In a study carried out in the early 1960s, Paul Mattingly attempted to trace fluctuations of the boundary of the CBD of Harrisburg, Pennsylvania, over the preceding 70 years.[1] Harrisburg was selected because it was considered not too large to work with (its urbanized area had a population of 210,000 in 1960) and because it seemed to have had several substantial changes in its primary direction of growth during the 70-year period.

1. Paul F. Mattingly, "Delimitation and Movement of CBD Boundaries Through Time: The Harrisburg Example," *The Professional Geographer* 16, no. 6 (November 1964): 9–13.

Mattingly decided to base his research on the Harrisburg CBDs for 1890, 1929, and 1960 and to use the CBI delimitation technique as far as possible. He had no difficulty in outlining the CBD for 1960 on this basis since current field mapping could be used, but the 1890 and 1929 CBDs were another matter. Fortunately, some land-use information is available on Sanborn fire insurance maps.[2]

However, it was found impossible to apply the standard CBI method for these earlier periods without some modification. The CBHI, important though it is in the technique, had to be eliminated, since land-use information was found not to be consistently obtainable on Sanborn maps for stories above the ground level. For the same reason, the CBII had to be based on ground-level use only. The CBD boundary lines used in the study are based on a CBII of 50 per cent as in the CBI delimitation, but this value is derived from the proportion of land occupied by central business activities at the ground-floor level only and not from land use of all floors. Still another adjustment had to be made: it was necessary to allow for changes in central business forms of land use throughout the 75 years, such as the switch from livery stables to parking lots.

When the Harrisburg CBD for 1960, delimited according to the regular CBI system, was compared with that resulting from use of Mattingly's modified system, it was found that the latter was ten blocks larger in area. The modified technique appears to have been less rigorous and of course it failed to take account of anything above the ground floor. Nevertheless, the method seems to have done a fair job of outlining the district and was used in delimiting all three of the Harrisburg CBDs compared by Mattingly, namely, those for 1890, 1920, and 1960.

Mattingly says that the present CBD of Harrisburg dates from about 1720 when John Harris, the founder of the city, constructed a trading post which was the original nucleus of the district. Without going into detail regarding the growth and shifts that followed, we can consider the boundary of 1890, the first year for which the attempt was made to determine the extent of the CBD.

At that time, Mattingly says, the district included 19 square blocks and extended almost the entire length of Market Street (Figs. 11.1 and 11.2). Most central business uses were found along Market Street and on intersecting streets where they joined it. Relatively few such activities were located on Walnut and Chestnut Streets. The principal factor focusing the CBD axis along Market Street seems to have been the early start of business on the end of the street nearest the Susquehanna River where there

---

2. Sanborn Fire Insurance Company maps show streets, railroad tracks, lot lines, dimensions of buildings, the nature of building materials, the number of stories, the uses of buildings, and certain other information. An atlas of Sanborn maps for the local city is likely to be available in realtors' offices, in offices dealing with fire insurance rating, in the city planning office, and at the county courthouse.

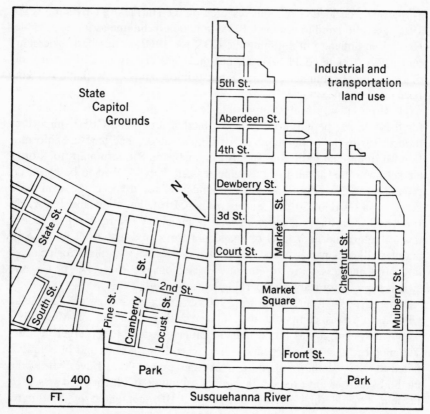

Source: Paul F. Mattingly, "Delimitation and Movement of CBD Boundaries through Time: The Harrisburg Example," *The Professional Geographer* 16 (1964), Fig. 2.

Fig. 11.1. Downtown Harrisburg, Pennsylvania, showing major streets and other features

was the combined stimulus of a bridge and of market houses that had been built in 1807. At the opposite end of Market Street were railroad passenger stations. Market Street was the most direct thoroughfare connecting these focal points of central business activity.

Between 1890 and 1929 the CBD continued to expand, adding an area of 11 square blocks on the east and a few more northwest of Walnut Street (Fig. 11.3). The causes for the directions of expansion cannot be traced in detail, but some of the reasons are clear. The market houses of Market Square were torn down in 1899, and there was a marked decline in business on Market Street as a result. The area of the CBD to the southeast of the Square then became the center of business, apparently due to the construction of two market houses at the corner of South Court and Chestnut Streets between 1890 and 1925. When this area became filled with estab-

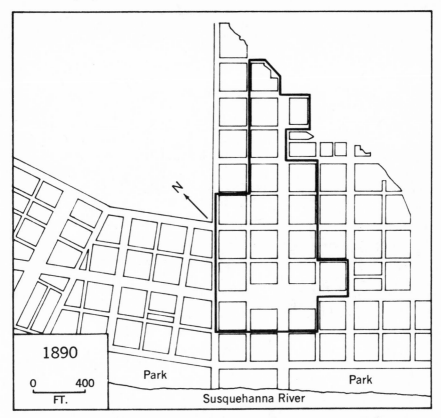

1890

0   400
FT.

Park

Park

Susquehanna River

Source: Paul F. Mattingly, "Delimitation and Movement of CBD Boundaries through Time: The Harrisburg Example," *The Professional Geographer* 16 (1964), Fig. 2.

Fig. 11.2. Downtown Harrisburg showing approximate CBD Boundary for 1890

lishments, the only direction for expansion was to the north and west of Walnut Street since a railroad line on the man-made ridge of Mulberry Street acted as a barrier to southeastward movement. Industrial and transportation land fulfilled the same function to the west and south. Only one direction was still open: north between the capitol grounds and Front Street.

Between 1929 and 1960 the CBD continued to grow northward from Walnut Street between the Susquehanna River and the capitol grounds. Ten blocks were added to the CBD in this region and seven in other directions, scattered around the CBD periphery (Fig. 11.4).

The present CBD shape reflects both natural and cultural forces. Natural barriers, other than the Susquehanna, have had little influence on the district's extent. Most of the land on which the CBD is situated slopes gently westward, from the hilltop on which the capitol buildings are located to

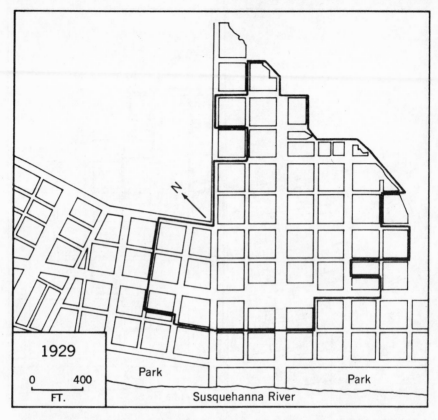

Source: Paul F. Mattingly, "Delimitation and Movement of CBD Boundaries through Time: The Harrisburg Example," *The Professional Geographer* 16 (1964), Fig. 2.

Fig. 11.3. Downtown Harrisburg showing approximate CBD boundary for 1929

the river. This slope has formed no significant barrier to development. But there are man-made barriers, including a wide expanse of railroad tracks toward the east, a rail line following the crest of the small man-made ridge of Mulberry Street, and the government buildings to the north. So there is only one direction in which further expansion is probable. This is between the capitol grounds and the Susquehanna River. There is evidence that the CBD is still shifting northward. On the other hand, the two major department stores in the downtown area are near the corner of Fourth and Market Streets where they appear to act as an anchor against the district's continued northward movement..

Mattingly's study dealt with changes through time and thus to some degree was historical, but the time period involved was limited and concern was chiefly with the changing CBD boundary. The next inquiry to be summarized is more definitely historical geography.

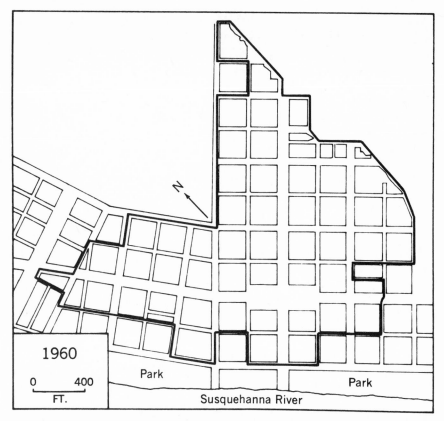

1960

0   400
FT.

Park

Park

Susquehanna River

Source: Paul F. Mattingly, "Delimitation and Movement of CBD Boundaries through Time: The Harrisburg Example," *The Professional Geographer* 16 (1964), Fig. 2.

Fig. 11.4. Downtown Harrisburg showing approximate CBD Boundary for 1960

Emergence of Boston's CBD

David Ward, in a paper published in 1966, discussed the effects of the Industrial Revolution on the dimensions and complexity of Boston's CBD.[3] It is not a study in techniques: Ward attempts no exact delimitation for any period nor any exact measurements. Rather, he presents a subjective analysis of progressive changes in the extent and character of central Boston. His work is presented in condensed form here, but enough is given to make clear the nature of the approach of the historical geographer to CBD study.

Ward points out that much of the internal complexity of many CBDs of today is rooted in changes associated with the Industrial Revolution. The

3. David Ward, "The Industrial Revolution and the Emergence of Boston's Central Business District," *Economic Geography* 42 (1966): 152–171.

large seaports of northeastern United States, he says, provide us with a good record of the distributional changes that took place within large cities during the period of rapid industrialization and immigration.

During the medieval period, European towns established street markets, and as time went on these facilities were improved and enlarged by the

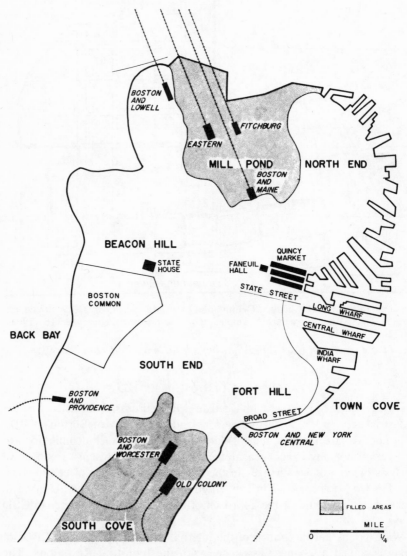

Source: David Ward, "The Industrial Revolution and the Emergence of Boston's Central Business District," *Economic Geography* 42 (1966), Fig. 1 (as generalized by Ward from Boynton Map of 1844 and Colton Map of 1855), p. 154.

Fig. 11.5. Commercial facilities in mid-nineteenth-century Boston

construction of market halls or warehouses. Many colonial American towns, including Boston, followed suit. But even as late as 1840, after several decades of commercial expansion, most of Boston's warehouses occupied a relatively small section of the waterfront to the south of State Street and the Long Wharf (Fig. 11.5). Local trade was conducted in the newly enlarged market facilities and from numerous small wharves north of State Street. Supplementing the market halls and waterfront establishments most merchants carried on business at their homes. Handicraft industries exhibited an increasing tendency to concentrate on particular streets, but in the early nineteenth century specialized manufacturing as well as specialized commercial activities (distribution, merchandising, and financing) occupied only small sections of the town. Most buildings and most districts were multifunctional.

Ward goes on to discuss the effect the railroads had on the expansion of specialized commercial development (Fig. 11.6). Boston's hilly, peninsular site created problems, such as a lack of space. Most railroads had to construct their terminals on filled land at some distance from the area of greatest commercial activity, the wharf area on the eastern side of the peninsula, where they found it nearly impossible to obtain sites on which to construct facilities of their own. The terminals to the south were separated from the existing nucleus of commercial activity by the residential districts of the South End and Fort Hill. Thus the railroad companies in Boston were at a disadvantage in having eight widely-scattered terminals.

The foreign commerce that had developed was based chiefly on the carrying trade, with little relation to the growing textile industry of Boston's immediate hinterland. Packet shipping, after a short trial of Boston's waterfront, sought terminal facilities in New York City, where access to the hinterland was better developed. Under these circumstances the new commercial facilities that did develop were close to the small but growing focus of financial and insurance operations on the upper end of State Street, which served the credit and informational requirements of the carrying trade.

In 1844 Boston housed 25 commercial banks, two savings banks, and 27 insurance companies; all but three were located on State Street. At first, the developments along State Street were, in many cases, located in buildings that had long combined the functions of residence and counting house. As more prosperous merchants moved into new homes in more exclusively residential neighborhoods, however, the original residences were converted into banks and insurance offices. Later they were demolished to make way for more specialized business structures. The old State Street area of Boston became exclusively financial. The location of this original nucleus of the financial district thus reflects an earlier residential area of men of wealth and influence.

The new financial quarter was situated near the market halls, but at some distance from the existing warehouses on the waterfront, and at an

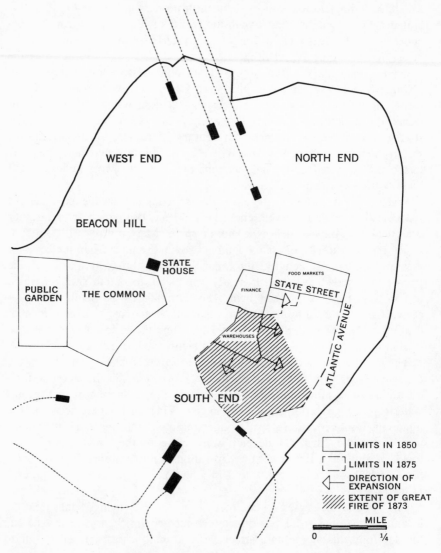

WEST END   NORTH END

BEACON HILL

STATE
HOUSE

FOOD MARKETS

PUBLIC
GARDEN   THE COMMON   FINANCE   STATE STREET

WAREHOUSES

ATLANTIC AVENUE

SOUTH END

☐ LIMITS IN 1850

[☐] LIMITS IN 1875

⟵ DIRECTION OF
    EXPANSION

////// EXTENT OF GREAT
////// FIRE OF 1873

MILE

0   ¼

Source: David Ward, "The Industrial Revolution and the Emergence of Boston's
Central Business District," *Economic Geography* 42 (1966), Fig. 3, p. 159.

Fig. 11.6. Expansion of Boston's CBD, 1850–1875

even greater distance from the railroad terminals in the Mill Pond and
South Cove areas (Fig. 11.7). After about 1830 nearly all the new warehouse construction in Boston took place on the southern margins of the
financial district and on State Street opposite the food markets. Their extent testified to the prosperity of Boston's carrying trade in the period just
before the Civil War. The location of the warehouse quarter, near the

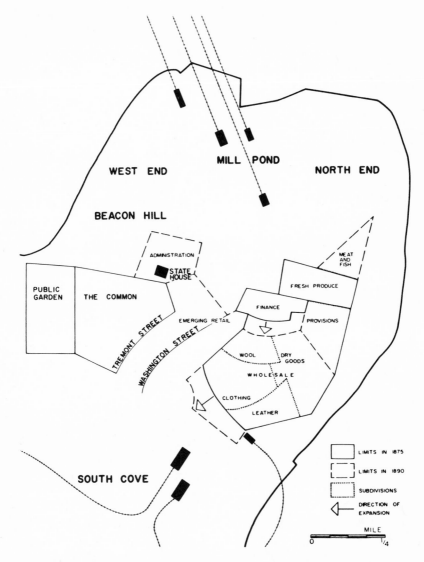

Source: David Ward, "The Industrial Revolution and the Emergence of Boston's Central Business District," *Economic Geography* 42 (1966), Fig. 4, p. 163.

Fig. 11.7. Expansion of Boston's CBD, 1875–1890

financial district and at considerable distance from existing waterfront and railroad terminals, showed the predominance of accessibility to informational and credit facilities over the desire for minimum transfer movements between terminals and warehouses.

With the depression of 1857, Boston's carrying trade declined, and, during the Civil War, British shipping cut even more deeply into the trade.

But other changes were under way. Clothing, footwear, and furniture manufacture had developed to serve the needs of the carrying trade for return commodities. Printing of advertisements and information had also become important. Such manufacturing as had developed consisted mostly of craft industries to begin with, but, during the fifties, workshops were established that employed unskilled workers in a minutely divided manufacturing process.

The lathe and sewing machine, and other technical innovations permitted expansion of such activities into the upper stories of warehouses, and even into the attics of adjacent tenements. But since control of the new workshops remained in the hands of the merchants, the various segments of the manufacturing process remained concentrated in the warehouse quarter. Since the market was elastic and uncertain, the nearness of this new manufacturing to the sources of credit and market information was advantageous.

Manufacturing activities thus supplemented merchandising and storage in the warehouse quarter, and stimulated even further southward expansion of the business district into adjacent residential areas. The surviving residences on Fort Hill and in the South End were converted into tenements, and open areas were soon filled with shacks which became a major immigrant focus within Boston. Then, in 1873, Boston's "Great Fire" consumed the south side of the warehouse district and obliterated all traces of the original residential function of the area. Civil authorities took this occasion to provide a new and wider pattern of streets and better regulation in general.

The removal of Fort Hill improved the accessibility of the warehouse district to South Cove railroad terminals, but immigrant housing still crowded in between the two areas. After a brief period of reconstruction following the Great Fire, the depression of the mid-seventies delayed further action for another generation. The need to regulate expansion of the warehouse district was likewise neglected.

The warehouse district, which was by far the largest segment of the CBD in 1875 (Fig. 11.7), continued to expand southward during the last decades of the nineteenth century. Increasingly, the warehouse premises were devoted to wholesale trade, as workshop manufacturing moved into new quarters and retailing assumed greater economic and locational autonomy. As local trade in dry goods and in food and provisions expanded, they required considerably enlarged accommodations for the central organization of regional distribution; so, too, did the wool and leather trades, which increased in volume as they served a far larger market than Boston's immediate hinterland.

Along with an increased business activity in Boston's CBD came a diminished emphasis upon manufacturing. Those workshop manufacturing industries that depended upon economies of rent could no longer afford warehouse accommodations. With the exception of certain sections of the printing industry, they adopted new quarters beyond the limits of the CBD. The footwear industry, for instance, was able to synchronize its production processes and reap economies of scale in large suburban factories. But the clothing industry, unable to enlarge its scale of operation, gravitated into the tenement districts of the North and West ends, where Jewish immigrants were available for the "sweat shops." The wholesale trade aspects of both the clothing and footwear manufacturing remained in the warehouse quarter (Fig. 11.7).

North of State Street, the market halls had provided cramped accommodations for the fresh food and provision trade. But, during the last quarter of the nineteenth century, the assembly and distribution of food grew in magnitude; so, as with dry goods, it differentiated into separate retail and wholesale segments. From the market halls trade in fresh food and provisions expanded along the waterfront both to the north and south of State Street, and in the process segregated into three specialized precincts. The original market halls concentrated on fresh produce, the waterfront to the north of the halls specialized on fish and meat, and the waterfront to the south handled and sold general provisions. By 1920 most wholesale food markets were located on the northern side of State Street and had invaded parts of the North End tenement quarter. This distinctive tenement area survived, furnishing much of the labor and later much of the management and ownership of the food trades.

Ward points out that the southward expansion of the warehouse district was also made necessary by the encroachments of the financial district on its northern margins. In 1875 financial activities were still concentrated on the south side of State Street, where they had first emerged in the thirties and forties. By 1895 the banks and insurance offices had spread into adjacent sections of the warehouse district. By 1920 even the wool warehouses had given way to financial activities (Fig. 11.8). Public administration and associated services had grown up in a small area around the State House, but by the end of the century they had spread southward to merge with the newly enlarged financial quarter.

Early in the nineteenth century this close association of administrative and financial functions had been separated by the establishment of new accommodations for state government on what was then the edge of town. By the turn of the century, expansion from separate nuclei resulted in a much more extensive area devoted to finance, administration, and associated professional services. Expansion of administrative and professional accommodations into adjacent residential areas was relatively restricted, for Beacon Hill, like the North End, proved to be an enduring residential district on the immediate edge of the business district. Beacon Hill housed native Americans of wealth and status, however, whereas the North End was inhabited by Italian immigrants. Thus the wholesale food markets and

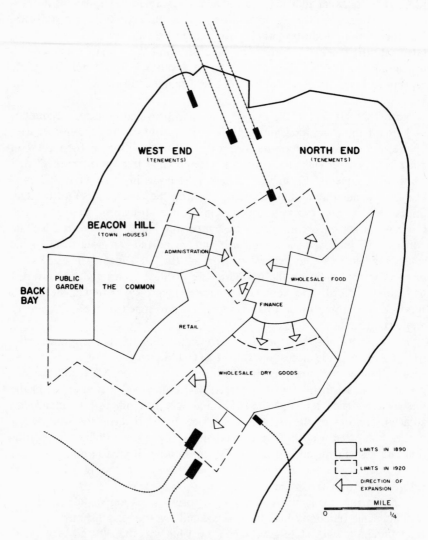

WEST END
(TENEMENTS)

NORTH END
(TENEMENTS)

BEACON HILL
(TOWN HOUSES)

ADMINISTRATION

PUBLIC
GARDEN

THE COMMON

WHOLESALE FOOD

BACK
BAY

FINANCE

RETAIL

WHOLESALE DRY GOODS

LIMITS IN 1890

LIMITS IN 1920

DIRECTION OF
EXPANSION

MILE

0   ¼

Source: David Ward, "The Industrial Revolution and the Emergence of Boston's Central Business District," *Economic Geography* 42 (1966), Fig. 5, p. 165.

Fig. 11.8. Expansion of Boston's CBD, 1890–1920

the administrative quarter of the business district were unable to extinguish the adjacent residential districts. Rather, they expanded into the area between State Street and the Mill Pond railroad terminals within which residences and businesses had for long been interspersed.

Until about 1880, Ward says, the distribution of dry goods was in the hands of the commission agents or merchants who controlled parts of the manufacturing process. The consumer either bought these goods directly from the warehouse or from a general store. In 1875, apart from custom retail trade within the financial district, there was no clearly defined, specialized retail section within the CBD devoted to ready-made consumer goods. But, during the eighties, falling retail prices made it increasingly necessary for merchants to take advantage of marginal economies. With the expansion of wholesale trade within the warehouse quarter many merchants began to establish showrooms and to develop direct selling to customers. These showrooms were situated in accessible and attractive parts of the central area of the city, concentrated between the warehouse quarter and the Common (see Fig. 11.7).

By 1890 most of the newly electrified streetcar services focused on this district, bringing access to the growing sources of employment in the CBD. It meant, too, much more retail activity for the district. The retail quarter housed two contrasting types of retail activity: (1) large-scale trade in a wide range of frequently needed items, and (2) sale of specialty items which were purchased less frequently but needed the newly enlarged threshold to survive.

Washington and Tremont Streets carried many of the streetcar lines into the central parts of the city, and it was on these two streets that most of the early retail stores first developed. Washington Street attracted large-scale or department stores, whereas more specialized and expensive items were retailed through premises on Tremont Street overlooking the Common. By 1920 the Common obstructed further expansion of the retail quarter in that part of the CBD which was also adjacent to the financial and warehouse districts. Retail premises expanded around the southern part of the Common and began to encroach upon the exclusive residential area of the Back Bay (see Fig. 11.8). In this way the prior claims and justly sentimental attachment of Bostonians to Boston Common removed from the market land that was appropriately located for retail purposes, thereby affecting the direction of expansion and the location of Boston's CBD.

By the turn of the century, the increase in the amount of local traffic on the CBD's narrow streets had created serious problems of congestion. The first major efforts to alleviate the growing congestion were made by the private streetcar company. A rapid transit system was constructed, consisting of an elevated track between two of Boston's inner suburbs adjacent to the edge of the CBD. This elevated track provided not only a more convenient and much faster service from the nearby suburbs to the CBD but also a loop line that linked various parts of the district. In order to provide access into the central part of the CBD, several subways were constructed between 1900 and 1915.

But the scale of improvements was quite inadequate, according to Ward, to meet the needs of daily commuters or to alleviate the increasing congestion within the business district. The construction of elevated tracks and subways demanded heavy capital expenditures by the company at a time when the process of electrification had only just been completed and when labor and material costs were rising rapidly. Alleviation of the congestion was thus delayed and limited by the economic dilemma of the transit system and by the failure of civil authorities to diagnose more accurately the causes of the difficulty.

Traffic congestion within Boston's CBD was intensified by the wide separation of railroad and waterfront terminal facilities. Public investigations of Boston's commercial predicament after the decline of the grain export trade focused attention upon the uncoordinated terminals' facilities, but rarely identified the needs of terminals to serve local as distinct from international trade. Most inquiries were preoccupied with the intractable problem of financing. But this was the first time the predicament of the modern business district was faced squarely, and even then only limited efforts were made to facilitate internal movement.

In his study, Ward was predominantly interested in the impact of the Industrial Revolution upon Boston's CBD, and he gave only small space to a discussion of the district's problem following 1920. His work did, however, set forth in considerable detail the changing emphasis from the seventeenth and eighteenth centuries until the early twentieth century. During this period, Boston's downtown evolved from the market halls and general waterfront warehousing of the early period to a greatly enlarged and crowded CBD, where such specialized functions as finance and retailing occupy much of the space.

Studies of Central Philadelphia

About the time that Murphy and Vance were doing their research on the nine CBDs, John Rannells was conducting an urban land-use investigation that focused on central Philadelphia.[4] His work will be briefly discussed here as well as a Philadelphia City Planning Commission report on central Philadelphia, from which Rannell's study derives.[5]

THE CORE OF THE CITY

In Rannells' *The Core of the City,* which focuses on Philadelphia, an unusual point of view is maintained. The center of interest is "activities," and "establishments," and these, rather than areas, are regarded as units of land use. According to the author, "individuals and establishments in action

4. John Rannells, *The Core of the City: A Pilot Study of Changing Land Uses in Central Business Districts* (New York: Columbia University Press, 1956).
5. Philadelphia City Planning Commission, *Philadelphia Central District Study* (prepared by Alderson and Sessions, Philadelphia, 1951).

make the city," (p. 17) and changing relationships between activities express themselves in changing demands for space—that is, changing locational demands.

Terminology plays an important role in the study. The changing patterns of urban land use are considered to result from the interplay of two elements: activities and physical accommodations. An "activities" approach to description of urban patterns is followed. An "establishment" is defined as a recognizable place of business, residence, government, or assembly. An example of a system of activity is a grocery chain in which the executive office, the meat-buying office, the dairy warehouse, each retail store, and so on are individual establishments. Physical accommodations are relatively permanent, whereas patterns of activity, with their myriad interrelationships, are ever changing. One example is the succession of establishments that may occupy a single building; another is the continuous shifting of establishments among available locations within the urban area.

The chief purpose of the study "is to establish a factual basis for analyzing phenomena of growth and change in the city center, with the goals of conserving and enhancing urban resources." (p. 51) It is achieved largely through setting up and employing three statistical measures of core characteristics: (1) an index of concentration, (2) a center of gravity, and (3) a radius of dispersion. These measures permit analysis of the extent of the district which is truly characterized by a major land use, where that use is centered, and the extent of its normal spread throughout the district. Rannells uses each of these statistical measures to point out successive locational characteristics of major land-use categories. A series of models is established for relationships among these use categories for 1934 and for 1949. A comparison of the two sets of models shows the character of change within the core.

Rannells' research focuses upon the Philadelphia city core, by implication the Philadelphia CBD. No special technique is used for the delimitation of such an area, however. As we have found so often in other cases, the CBD extent seems just to have been assumed, possibly because no comparisons with CBDs of other cities were involved. Before turning to the Philadelphia situation, the author discusses the factors to which may be attributed the arrangement of uses within the CBD, or in any other urban area for that matter. These "systems of action" help to answer the question "Where do things belong in an urban area?" The systems are concerned with urban activities on three levels: that of the individual, that of the grouping of individuals or the "establishment," and that of the relationship between establishments, "linkages." The establishments are the basis for the study of location and the linkages for a study of transportation relationships among establishments.

Unlike most of the studies summarized in this book, *The Core of the City* concentrates on theory and techniques but offers little by way of substantive findings. It does not add much to our knowledge of CBDs, not even that of central Philadelphia, but presumably further study along the lines proposed should lead to a deeper understanding of the land use complexities of the CBD.

A PLANNING STUDY OF CENTRAL PHILADELPHIA

Rannells, before working on *The Core of the City,* had been associated with Alderson and Sessions in their planning study of central Philadelphia for the Philadelphia City Planning Commission. Working for the Planning Commission, the firm produced a report which has often been referred to in the literature as the "Philadelphia Central District Study" or as the "Philadelphia CBD Study." Data assembled in connection with the study formed the basis for Rannells' graphic and statistical techniques, but their study had objectives of its own. The Philadelphia Central District Study followed what has been called "the space-use method" with the purpose of forecasting the demand for space in the central district of Philadelphia in 1960 and 1980 by kinds of space. In so doing the Central District or CBD was defined "broadly in an attempt to include the great majority of establishments which are oriented toward a broader area than their immediate neighborhoods."[6] (p. 2)

The inventory of total space in the Philadelphia Central District was prepared for 1934 and 1949, covering all space designed for nonresidential use. Establishments were divided into six basic land-use types: (1) retailing, (2) manufacturing, (3) wholesaling with stocks, (4) wholesaling without stocks, (5) business services, and (6) consumer services. A second grouping was made for functional combinations, namely, manufacturing and wholesaling with stocks; business services and wholesaling without stocks; and retailing and consumer services. A third grouping, according to movement problems, involved just two categories: goods-handling establishments (retailing, manufacturing, and wholesaling with stocks); and non-goods-handling establishments (consumer services, business services, and wholesaling without stocks.)

Analyzing the change in Philadelphia's Central District for the 15-year period between 1934 and 1949, the report considered both the number of establishments and the floor space occupied. On these bases, they found that "retailers and manufacturers became fewer but larger on the average; and only wholesaling increased in both dimensions, but within wholesaling, nearly all the increase in numbers was in wholesaling without stocks." (p. 24)

6. The Central District was defined geographically as "the area lying between the Delaware and Schuykill Rivers and running from Green Street on the north to Bainbridge Street on the south. This area comprises 3.12 square miles . . ."

Methods of Study of CBD Change

It is much easier to map and analyze the static CBD than CBD change. Nevertheless, CBDs do not stand still; it is important to study the district's changing picture. By what methods is CBD change studied?

Ratcliff and Foley, as described in Chapter 10, made practical applications of the idea of CBD change. Ratcliff, in studying functional change in the Madison CBD, outlined two areas: Area A, a sort of retail core, and Area B, the remainder of central Madison. Using city directories he recorded land uses for the two areas at five-year intervals to determine the overall functional changes for the 30-year period ending in 1950. Note that Ratcliff used only arbitrarily chosen boundaries, the same boundaries for the entire period, thus taking no account of possible changes in the extent of his "central business area" during the 30 years.

Foley, in trying to determine whether or not offices had been suburbanizing in the San Francisco Bay Area, used no fixed boundaries for his study area but merely concentrated on the downtown sections of San Francisco and adjacent smaller cities. He concerned himself particularly with changes in the 25-year period from 1928 to 1954, and obtained his information through telephoning Bay Area firms, through personal interviews with executives, and from reports on other metropolitan areas and discussions of their problems. Neither Ratcliff nor Foley restricted his work to any very exactly defined CBD.

The studies of Mattingly and Ward, described in the present chapter, had no such practical purposes as the two research projects just described. Through a modification of the CBI technique, Mattingly outlined the Harrisburg CBD for 1890, 1929, and 1960 on comparable bases, and thus was able to study the district's shifts in position and to speculate on the reasons for the shifts. Ward's work was more completely historical geography. In studying the evolution of the Boston CBD, he made no attempt to delimit the district or even to describe its extent in at all precise terms. Instead, he emphasized progressive changes in the evolution and character of the CBD, leaving the changing position of its boundary largely to inference on the part of the reader.

The fifth study of the group, that of Rannells working in Philadelphia, is hardly comparable to the others mentioned since it deals largely with methods by which change could be studied rather than a specific case of change.

But there are other ways of studying CBD change. For instance, land use can be compared for two periods using the regular CBI technique to outline successive CBD extents, and a quantitative expression of change worked out. The current land-use mapping is simple, of course, but it is difficult to produce a land-use map of reasonable accuracy for the same general area for the earlier period in order to arrive at really comparable delimitations and measurements of land-use changes.

Another possibility of studying CBD change was referred to in Chapter 7, that presented by Census CBDs. Since census tracts normally are the same in extent from one decennial census to the next they would seem to be ideal for measuring changes in the CBD. Census CBDs *are* of value in determining changes in sales or other comparable business data from one business census to the next. And ordinary census tract data, too, as given in decennial censuses of population and housing, are available for Census CBDs. But this brings us back to an evaluation of the Census CBD. It is satisfactory as a census tract or group of such tracts for recording business data and even for studying changes in such data from one Census of Business to another. But it is a poor expression of the morphological unit or geographic region that has become known as the central business district of the city.

12

The CBD and the Future

In this final chapter, any of several courses might be pursued. In view of the nature of the book it would seem logical to concentrate further on the research that has been done and the queries regarding the CBD that present the greatest challenges for further research. But the various lines of attack followed have already been discussed and attention called to questions that particularly need to be answered.

This chapter will focus, instead, on the future of the CBD. It is not an outgrowth of the research discussed throughout the book, but attempts to answer a quite separate and independent question: What's happening to the district and what is likely to happen? Some general background will be presented and views of several students of the city who are known for their vigorous opinions regarding the area's prospects. What effect is urban renewal having upon the CBD? This too has to be considered. With this background of opinions and information, together with his own views, the author will attempt to outline something of the CBD's probable future.

What's Happening to the CBD?

A number of people have given serious attention to the question of what is happening to the CBD in the United States. The areal restriction is intentional since the forces that affect the American CBD are unlikely to operate in exactly the same manner in another country.

GENERAL BACKGROUND [1]

To many urban planners and other students of the city, the future of the metropolis depends upon the future of downtown: the two are inseparable.

---

1. This section is based in considerable part upon John C. Bollens and Henry J. Schmandt, *The Metropolis: its People, Politics, and Economic Life,* 2nd ed. (New York: Harper & Row, Publishers, 1970), pp. 90–97.

The CBD, they say, is the real heart of the city, the focal point around which the activities of the metropolis revolve. There can be no prosperous city without a successful downtown. Let this hub deteriorate and the metropolis will be sapped of strength and vigor.

Other observers take exactly the opposite view. They think the CBD has ceased to serve a useful purpose. Should we spend millions of dollars each year, they ask, to pump vitality into an "obsolete and outmoded appendage"? Such attempts, these people think, are unrealistic. The community should free itself of its long-standing commitment to the preservation of the CBD and devote its resources to alternative possibilities.

Still other students of the city, a third group, take a more moderate though critical stand. They consider the CBD to be on trial but by no means convicted. Acknowledging the crucial importance of the downtown, they nevertheless criticize city planners and administrators for their failure to recognize its changing role and to act accordingly.

In any event it must be admitted that the residents of the metropolitan area, particularly of the principal central city, have a large stake in the CBD. It represents a huge investment of community wealth and a correspondingly large source of tax revenue for the local government. Within the CBD is the area's greatest concentration of office buildings, department stores, specialty shops, hotels, financial institutions, and governmental agencies. It is the center of the transportation and communications networks of the metropolis. In fact, by almost any test that can be applied it is hard to ignore the leading role of the CBD in the life of the metropolis.

The CBD is considered to offer unique advantages in three functional areas: (1) furnishing specialized and comparison shopping; (2) providing office facilities for the so-called "confrontation" industries; and (3) servicing the small businesses and industries that seek the economies which concentration offers.[2]

The chief advantage that the CBD is said to retain in the retail sector is the opportunity for specialized and comparison shopping. This applies chiefly to large cities, however, since there must be a large aggregation of department stores and specialty shops in order to provide depth and variety of merchandise and a range of choice in brand, style, quality, and price. And this advantage is now being challenged by the development of larger regional shopping centers which themselves offer comparison shopping opportunities.

When we look at the situation with respect to standardized goods, the difference is immediately apparent. Since these can be procured in any neighborhood or regional shopping center, the CBD has tended to lose this sort of business. However, the downtown can still count on a large

2. John C. Bollens and Henry J. Schmandt, *The Metropolis: its People, Politics, and Economic Life,* 2nd ed. (New York: Harper & Row, Publishers, 1970), pp. 94–95.

clientele of office workers, government employees, and others who are in the CBD for purposes other than shopping. And it has some new markets for these more ubiquitous items. A local clientele of some size is being created in the larger SMSAs as a result of the luxury apartments that are appearing in or near the CBDs of our larger cities on land made available largely through urban renewal projects.

"Confrontation" industries are the financial institutions and business offices, particularly headquarters offices, which tend to cluster in the CBDs of large cities. They cluster partly because of the advantages of direct negotiation and conferring. And advertising agencies, accounting firms, office suppliers, and other service providers find it advantageous to locate in the same area as their major clients and customers. It is said that, in the CBD, opportunities for lunch-hour shopping, for after-hours recreation and entertainment, and for meeting people continue to be the best available anywhere in the urban area.

The CBD is considered to offer locational advantages, too, for small plants and businesses which produce nonstandard products and are dependent on the use of "external" facilities or services.[3] But these favorable circumstances are limited chiefly to downtown sections of New York and other very large cities.

VANCE'S VIEWS OF CBD CHANGE[4]

Against this broad background of what's happening to the CBD we may look at several more specific opinions. J. E. Vance, Jr., points out that since World War II virtually all growth in the metropolitan commercial structure has taken place outside the CBD, but that the core is changing rather than decaying. The central business district, he says, "has become the mass seller to the inner part of the metropolis, the specialty seller to the geographical city, and the office area for the region." (p. 518)

Vance predicts that the CBD "will continue to exist but shorn of much of its former purpose." (p. 517) Already it is thought of more and more as a place of offices rather than of large stores. The focus of metropolitan arteries along with the functional convenience of integration of offices will tend, he says, to maintain the financial sub-district at the core. In some cities this focus of offices is being reinforced by introduction of rapid transit. But the presence of a mass transit system is no advantage to the retail sub-district. Shoppers now visit the downtown infrequently and when they do they prefer the flexibility of driving. The best location for the specialty shops which remain in the CBD is not in the area of office concentration with its congestion and pre-empted parking.

3. See discussion of external economies in Chapter 9.
4. J. E. Vance, Jr., "Emerging Patterns of Commercial Structure in American Cities," Proceedings of the IGU Symposium in Urban Geography, Lund, 1960, *Lund Studies in Geography,* series B, *Human Geography,* no. 24 (1962), 485–518.

Vance sees a trend toward two downtowns, possibly with a band of parking between. The single focus of the past may be lost, he thinks, and we may in the future have to limit the term "central business district" to the office area, with some name such as "metropolitan specialty district" for the other downtown focus.

ULLMAN'S VIEWS ON THE CBD[5]

Edward Ullman begins by pointing out the relative loss of SMSA retail trade suffered by CBDs in recent decades. Of course this is a phenomenon that has been recognized for some time, but Ullman carries the story further by calling attention to the low-income "gray area" typically occurring around the CBD. Urban renewal is pushed in these poor areas in part as a means of providing CBD customers, he says. In addition, a market for high and medium income apartments can be developed around downtowns, but he doubts if this market is very great in most cities.

The remaining large activity for CBDs, Ullman says, is the office function. This is growing in great cities, particularly in New York City which has witnessed a boom in central office construction. To a degree it is happening in Washington, D.C., too. But the only cities likely to participate in the office expansion are the large ones and particularly those that become international or regional office management or financial centers. Chicago's expansion and planned new construction will not result in any substantial increase in *per capita* office space though it will help the Loop. Rapid office growth has been going on, too, in Los Angeles, Detroit, and several other great cities.

In some cities, according to Ullman, outlying office centers are starting to develop, as seen in Los Angeles and St. Louis. In the latter the development is in Clayton, some distance west of the CBD. Actually, Clayton is nearer the city's geographic center than is the CBD and nearer the high income area of the city and the homes of its executives. It has many modern office buildings, both city-wide and country-wide in scope, which command rents as much as three times those of downtown. Ancillary businesses and social services, too, have sprung up. The Clayton center is not as large as downtown St. Louis, of course, but the area is within easy driving distance of the downtown for conferences.

A recent news item suggests that the surburban development of offices in St. Louis may represent more than a local trend. In Dallas the pace of office building in the downtown has been declining while large suburban office construction projects have been announced. Factors underlying the shift in emphasis are said to include easy transportation access to the suburban areas, the ability to create a more attractive environment of workers,

5. Edward L. Ullman, "Presidential Address: The Nature of Cities Reconsidered," *The Regional Science Association, Papers and Proceedings* (1962): 7–23.

reduced land investment costs, and more architectural flexibility than is possible downtown.

Ullman says that many activities are downtown more or less by the accident of original location, or perhaps in response to linkages that disappeared years ago. The average downtown must be greatly improved if it is to compete successfully with new sites made available by modern transportation. This will be increasingly difficult with the outward movement of housing, retail trade, manufacturing, and other activities which now begin to reinforce each other elsewhere in outer portions of the urban area.

He says it appears that the CBD may become one of many centers. It may be the most important of these centers, but it will be less important relatively than in the past. It may well become "the shopping center for the large, low-income area around it and an office center on a reduced scale for older activities or smaller concerns needing poor, vacant space or using large amounts of cheap labor." (p. 21) The high-grade activities that have been characteristic of the top hierarchical position of the CBD will, Ullman says, abandon it for centers better located to serve the high income areas.

Other centers, he thinks, will develop on a regional or specialized basis in accordance with the multiple nuclei concept. He goes on to suggest how this concept may operate. One such center may well be at or near the airport which will be convenient for conventions and out-of-town visitors. Outlying shopping centers and centers for special entertainment, education, culture, and recreation will be scattered over the city wherever they are needed.

He questions the often-expressed tenet that a city cannot exist without a heart, the CBD. The metropolis of today, Ullman says, is not just one city but a federation of general and special centers. It is likely eventually to have several hearts better located than the present one and be basically better off because of the reduction in travel time and congestion and through utilization of better sites.

Ullman says that if we were to start over we probably would not build our cities as they are today. But we go on reinforcing our mistakes. Urban renewal focusing on the CBD is subsidized, and priority is given to a radial pattern for the interstate highway system focused on the downtown.

HOMER HOYT AND THE CBD [6]

Homer Hoyt, a well-known urban planner, reinforces what Ullman says regarding the increasing importance of office buildings in the CBD. Pointing out how the CBD has changed from what was described by Burgess in the 1920s (see Chapter 1), he says that it is still the largest shopping district

6. Homer Hoyt, "Recent Distortions of the Classical Models of Urban Structure," *Land Economics* 40 (1964): 199–212.

but that it has lost in its proportion of the urban area's total business. This is due to the growth of planned shopping districts, especially the regional shopping center, in the city's periphery and in the suburbs, a development that can be traced in large part to the automobile. In a few cases, the downtown has been improved through the building of expressways which have resulted in the construction of new stores, but this has been the exception.

Hoyt goes on to tell how offices have multiplied in the downtown centers of a few of our largest cities owing to their significance as international or regional centers. This office construction in many cases has been associated with urban renewal, its location determined in part by slums and blighted areas, in part by old buildings which could be razed. But it is hard to generalize about offices and CBDs. In many cities of growing population few new office buildings are being erected, and in others new offices are going up inside the city but outside the CBD, even in outlying shopping centers.

An interesting point in connection with this suburbanization is the tendency for large office buildings of insurance companies, which conduct operations not dependent upon contacts with other agencies, to be located on tracts several miles from the center of the city. Office centers are also said to be developing around some of the regional shopping centers such as at Northland in Detroit and Ward Parkway in Kansas City. Hoyt says that while the main office building district of the average great city is still in the central area the center of gravity of offices is not fixed but tends to move toward the city's high income areas.

In some cities of only moderate size, as in Providence, Rhode Island, office buildings are going up in areas of established demand and hence generally within the CBD. And occasionally in an even smaller city a tall office building may loom up, built by a bank, an oil company, or an insurance company, often for reasons of prestige, regardless of cost or rental demand.

Hoyt points out, too, the decline in the importance of central hotels, owing to the growth of new motels and motor hotels on the periphery of the CBD and in the outskirts of the city. This development could not have been anticipated when Burgess developed his concentric zone idea, nor could the rise of apartments in or near the CBD, nor the effect of urban renewal in mitigating the slum conditions in areas which bordered the CBD in the 1920s.

URBAN RENEWAL AND THE CBD

Another aspect of the CBD story to keep in mind is urban renewal. When people talk about what is going to happen to the downtown it is now taken for granted that the CBD will have urban renewal in progress. It is the method by which a chronic CBD problem, growing obsolescence, is being met. Urban renewal is likely to be under way in the poorest sections of the CBD and in the "gray" zone at the district's edge.

There are difficulties encountered in urban renewal in the CBD that sometimes slow down the process. Among them are divided ownership and absentee ownership of sites. Even more serious are problems of a social nature that arise. Is adequate provision made for resettlement of the low-income residents who have been occupants of the renewal area? But in spite of these difficulties and others, urban renewal is proceeding in many CBDs and whether right or wrong is doing much to sustain downtown business.

Looking Forward

The future of the CBD has been a cause for concern on the parts of many planners and others interested in the welfare of the city. As brought out in earlier pages of this chapter, diverse conclusions have been reached as to the importance of the district and as to how it should be treated. Many people would like to be able to envision the CBD of 50 or even 25 years hence, and the district's future is indeed a matter of practical importance. To the proprietor of a CBD store, burdened with high property taxes and increasing competition from suburban businesses, it's a question of whether to hold on or not; to the real estate speculator it's a gamble on the CBD future; to the city administrator it's the problem of trying best to fit the CBD into plans for the city.

In spite of spending many years concentrating on the CBD both in his own research and through that of others, the author of this book claims no second sight concerning the future of the district, no crystal ball from which he can read the answers; and he is well aware that nothing he concludes can represent a venture into virgin territory. But still there remains the question: What is the CBD's probable future? A certain summing up of the facts of the case is in order.

Several types of establishments have been leaving the CBD and probably will continue to do so. For some time the district has been losing in relative importance in retailing due to the rise of suburban shopping centers. It may mean at first only that a downtown department store establishes a branch in the shopping center, but the suburban development is often much more directly competitive than this. The situation is really serious where some of the big, new regional shopping centers are developing, since they have enough large stores to compete successfully with the downtown in comparison shopping, which has normally been considered a CBD perquisite. The current dependence upon the automobile and the availability of vast parking areas at shopping centers are all-important elements of the situation.

What other businesses are on the move? Hotels are a type in which the CBD has certainly been losing out. In very large cities, downtown hotels will remain, but in cities of moderate size they are disappearing. So many travelers come by car nowadays that motels, chiefly in suburban areas, are taking over this type of service. To a lesser extent banks are decentralizing by establishing branches in city suburbs. However, such branches seldom are very large and each tends to serve only a limited portion of the metropolitan area.

A third type of business that is leaving the downtown is the insurance office. Insurance companies have been moving their main office establishments to the suburbs and will probably continue to do so. They are generally self-sufficient enough not to be dependent upon the contacts with other agencies and offices that the CBD affords and hence can take advantage of the economies of a less central location.

Other examples of businesses that are succumbing to the lure of the suburban shopping center are not hard to find. Certainly, there is ample reason for observers to feel that most expansion of the city's commercial structure in the future is likely to occur outside the city core.

But there are some lines of activity in which CBDs are gaining. There are, for example, large, medium, and high priced apartment houses which are being built at the edge of the CBD in very large cities, and their occupants are likely to be part of the clientele of CBD stores. And some, but by no means all, CBDs are acquiring more offices. This is especially true of CBDs in large cities that are significant as international and regional centers. But even in the large cities the picture isn't all one of CBD gain. There is a distinct tendency today, instead of crowding more offices into the downtown of some of the largest cities, to consider building the offices farther toward the edges of the city or in the suburbs.

Although the "gray" margins of the CBD frequently are written off as a loss, a recent study suggests that this judgment is too hasty, that they, even without urban renewal, are a flexible resource of floor space available for a mixture of certain uses that seem to do well along the edge of the district. Most of the buildings are of substantial construction and the floor space is low-cost and often easily adaptable.

Some of the most critical problems of the CBD normally have to do with access and parking. City after city is struggling to make its CBD accessible and to furnish adequate customer parking. Today, a CBD of any substantial size will certainly have at least one pedestrian mall and maybe more. Some planners are now talking of making all the downtown streets pedestrian malls with parking garages around the periphery and possibly even moving-sidewalks for the pedestrians.

The CBD is by no means dead. It is alive and generally is considered worth keeping alive. In spite of obsolescence, it represents a huge investment of community wealth and an important source of tax revenue for the city government. No, the CBD is not dying nor decaying, but it is changing. Will it become two centers as Vance thinks? Or a number of centers as suggested by Ullman? Changes such as these come slowly and it is likely that the CBD will remain much as it is today for some years to come, though with a still further mild decline in retailing and perhaps some increase in offices. Locally, however, there will be changes in the geography of individual CBDs. Urban renewal never spreads its blessings evenly, and within the CBD of your city some areas probably will wax as others wane.

In any event it is an interesting thought that we are subsidizing the CBD through urban renewal and thus from federal government money and city taxes. Urban renewal is a sort of shot in the arm for the district. The cost represents what society is willing to pay to keep an economically healthy downtown. But is it necessary? We are supporting downtown properties which are, presumably, making money for their owners, and we are doing it in part because it is generally assumed that a vigorous downtown is necessary for a prosperous city. But do we know this? From the opinions of the commentators whose ideas were presented earlier in this chapter it might be concluded that we are backing a losing cause, that the CBD is doomed to break up eventually. If so, why subsidize it? But in the meanwhile we are doing so, and thus, no doubt, staying the district's natural tendency to decline.

In the opinion of the author the future of the CBD is by no means a bleak one. Though losing retail trade and certain other businesses to suburbia the region has advantages no other section of the metropolis can offer. It will continue to have an accessibility that will keep many functions there; and the concentration of office buildings, financial institutions, department stores, and related service facilities within the CBD provides a business environment that would be difficult to duplicate anywhere else in the metropolis. After all it *is* the best locality for serving the entire urban area.

Appendix A

Field data for the nine CBDs delimited by Murphy and Vance

	Grand Rapids	Mobile	Phoenix	Roanoke	Sacra-mento	Salt Lake City	Tacoma	Tulsa	Worcester	Average
Gross area of CBD (acres)	97.3	73.0	126.7	77.4	188.2	189.4	67.8	136.3	87.1	115.9
Ground-floor area (acres)	58.9	50.4	76.8	53.3	108.8	120.8	52.4	79.8	59.6	73.4
Total height index	3.320	2.124	1.806	2.337	2.009	2.114	2.336	3.154	2.964	2.422
Central Business Height Index	2.4	1.5	1.5	1.9	1.5	1.5	1.9	2.6	2.0	1.8
Central Business Intensity Index	72.9	70.5	82.0	82.8	73.1	73.0	80.5	82.5	67.9	76.0
Total floor space in CBD (acres)	195.5	107.1	138.8	124.5	228.4	255.4	122.4	251.8	176.7	177.8
Central business floor space in CBD (acres)	142.5	75.5	113.8	103.1	167.0	186.4	98.6	207.7	120.0	135.0
Average block size (acres)	1.73	2.02	2.13	1.72	2.13	6.71	1.59	1.86	2.13	2.45
Gross land area of CBD as percentage of area of incorporated city	.65	.45	1.16	.46	1.74	.55	.22	.80	.37	.71
Gross land area of CBD as percentage of area of urbanized area	.33	.28	.36	.35	.71	.40	.17	.56	.31	.39

Source: Based on mapping in the early 1950s.

Appendix B

Background data for the nine CBD cities, 1960

	Grand Rapids	Mobile	Phoenix	Roanoke	Sacramento	Salt Lake City	Tacoma	Tulsa	Worcester	Average
Incorporated city, area in sq. mi. (1960)	24.4	152.9	187.4	26.0	45.1	56.1	47.5	47.8	37.0	69.4
Incorporated city, population in thousands (1960)	177	203	439	97	192	189	148	262	187	210
Urbanized area, area in sq. mi. (1960)	91.2	171.5	24.8	40.4	134.0	132.0	82.8	70.2	61.3	89.8
Urbanized area, population in thousands (1960)	294	269	552	125	452	349	215	299	225	309
Percentage of urbanized area population inside central city (1960)	60.3	75.6	79.6	77.8	42.4	54.3	68.8	87.5	82.8	69.9
SMSA, area in sq. mi. (1960)	862	1242	9226	303	983	764	1676	3824	428	214
SMSA, population in thousands (1960)	363	314	664	159	503	383	322	419	323	383

Wholesale trade of U.A., employees (1960)	5463	3451	9358	2004	6029	7532	2800	7065	3345	5227
Retail trade of U.A., employees (1960)	17387	14963	34157	8116	25835	22386	12137	18771	13056	18534
Clerical and kindred workers in U.A. (1960)	16783	15306	31193	7996	35867	23796	11758	21771	14659	19903
Sales workers in U.A. (1960)	10589	6435	18568	4599	13649	11730	6300	10992	7027	9988
Wholesale trade of incorporated city, employees (1960)	3203	2972	7807	1649	2795	4446	2012	6404	2726	3779
Retail trade of incorporated city, employees (1960)	11193	11520	27596	6567	12143	13103	8694	16933	10802	13172
Clerical and kindred workers in incorporated city (1960)	11156	12924	25637	6270	18223	15199	8676	20086	12072	14471
Sales workers in incorporated city (1960)	6518	5247	14850	3709	6182	6963	4290	10032	5623	7046

RETAIL BUSINESS USES

Automotive										
AA —automobile sales— new and used	.7	—	2.8	.1	3.5	1.3	3.8	2.9	.4	1.7
AB —service station or garage	.5	.6	2.9	1.9	1.9	2.2	1.3	.7	.1	1.3.
AC —accessory, tire, and battery sales	1.0	.6	.3	.4	.7	.8	.6	.6	.1	.6
AD —automotive rental	.4	—	1.1	a	—	.3	.1	.1	.6	.3
A —totals	2.6	1.2	7.1	2.5	6.1	4.6	5.8	4.3	1.2	3.9
Variety										
VA —department store	7.1	10.3	8.4	7.5	2.9	5.3	7.5	5.2	9.3	7.1
VB —"5 and 10"	1.6	2.7	2.0	1.9	.8	1.1	1.5	.7	2.7	1.7
VC —drug store	.4	.3	.6	.5	.4	.6	.6	.5	.4	.5
VD —cigar and news	a	.2	.3	a	.2	a	.3	.1	.2	.2
V —totals	9.2	13.5	11.3	10.0	4.3	7.1	9.9	6.5	12.6	9.5
Miscellaneous										
MA —sport, photo, hobby, toy, etc.	.6	.8	1.0	.7	1.0	1.2	1.0	.4	.8	.8
MB —jewelry and gift	.5	.6	1.2	.5	.8	.8	.9	.4	.4	.7
MC —florist shop	.1	.1	.1	.2	a	.1	.2	.1	.2	.1
MD —book store	.1	a	.1	a	.1	.1	.2	.1	.1	.1
ME —office machine and furniture	.4	.3	.1	.2	.3	.8	.8	.5	.3	.4
MF —office supply and stationery	a	.8	.4	.6	.1	.3	.9	.8	.6	.5
MG —pawn shop	—	.3	.2	.3	.6	.3	.3	.2	a	.3
MH —amusement establishment	2.8	2.8	2.1	2.7	3.1	1.8	2.6	.9	2.8	2.4
M —totals	4.6	5.8	5.2	5.3	6.1	5.4	6.9	3.4	5.3	5.3

aLess than 0.1 per cent.

*Land occupied by tracks was not measured.

For each city, 100 per cent is total floor space in the CBD, defined in the study as the ground-floor area of all blocks that lay inside the boundaries of the CBD minus alleys and plus the areas of all upper floors. A dash indicates that no value was recorded. (Based on field work and office calculations in 1952–1953 as reported by Murphy, Vance, and Epstein in *Central Business District Studies*, Worcester, Mass., 1955.)

Appendix C

Detailed land-use proportions in percentages for each of the nine CBDs studied

	Grand Rapids	Mobile	Phoenix	Roanoke	Sacramento	Salt Lake City	Tacoma	Tulsa	Worcester	Average
Food										
FA —restaurant	1.0	1.9	2.0	1.3	3.1	1.8	1.8	1.6	1.5	1.8
FB —supermarket	.1	—	—	.6	.4	.2	.2	a	.9	.3
FC —general food	.1	.1	.4	.1	.1	.1	a	a	.2	.1
FD —food specialty	.2	.4	1.1	2.2	.6	.3	1.8	.2	.3	.8
FE —delicatessen and ice cream parlor	a	.1	—	.2	—	—	—	—	.1	.1
FF —package store	—	a	—	.1	.4	—	.1	—	—	.1
FG —bars	.2	—	.2	a	2.6	1.1	1.6	.4	.1	.7
F —totals	1.6	2.6	3.7	4.6	7.2	3.5	5.6	2.4	3.1	3.9
Clothing										
CA —women's clothing	1.7	3.2	1.8	1.6	1.2	1.6	1.7	1.0	1.8	1.7
CB —men's clothing	.9	.7	1.0	1.8	1.4	1.4	1.5	.9	.9	1.2
CC —family clothing	.2	.3	.4	.8	.4	.2	.4	.5	.1	.4
CD —clothing specialty	.6	—	.2	.6	.7	.5	.4	.1	.6	.4
CE —general shoe store	.1	.2	1.1	.7	.5	.2	.7	.1	.4	.4
CF —men's and women's clothing	—	.3	—	a	—	—	—	.4	.4	.1
C —totals	3.5	4.7	4.5	5.6	4.2	3.9	4.7	3.0	4.2	4.2
Household										
HA —furniture	2.2	2.3	1.3	5.1	3.5	2.9	3.4	2.4	2.7	2.9
HB —hardware and appliance	1.6	3.4	.9	3.9	2.0	1.8	2.6	1.0	.5	2.0
HC —dry goods, rugs, curtains, etc.	.2	.1	.2	.4	.4	.4	.2	a	.2	.2
HD —coal, oil, ice, and heating sales	—	.3	.1	.1	—	—	.3	—	.2	.1
HE —used furniture and antiques	—	—	.1	.1	.1	.5	.1	a	a	.1
H —totals	4.0	6.1	2.6	9.5	6.0	5.6	6.6	3.6	3.7	5.3

RETAIL BUSINESS USES

Appendix C · continued

	Grand Rapids	Mobile	Phoenix	Roanoke	Sacra-mento	Salt Lake City	Tacoma	Tulsa	Worces-ter	Average
Financial										
BA —bank	1.4	1.1	2.5	.8	1.7	1.0	1.8	1.4	2.1	1.5
BB —personal loan	.2	.8	.7	.2	.1	.7	.2	.4	.3	.4
BC —insurance agencies and real estate offices	.7	.9	1.2	.8	1.6	.4	.8	.4	1.0	.9
BD —brokers, stock, etc.	a	.1	.2	—	.1	.9	a	.1	.2	.2
B —totals	2.4	2.9	4.6	1.8	3.5	3.0	2.9	2.3	3.6	3.0
Service Trades										
TA —personal service	1.6	1.5	2.7	4.8	1.6	1.4	1.4	.9	3.1	2.1
TB —clothing service	1.0	.4	.8	.7	1.1	.8	.7	.5	.4	.7
TC —household service	a	a	.1	a	.2	.1	a	.1	a	.1
TD —business service	a	a	.1	.8	.2	.2	.3	.1	.4	.2
TF —newspaper publishing	1.0	—	1.2	1.9	.6	1.7	.4	.5	1.1	1.0
T —totals	3.7	2.1	4.9	8.3	3.7	4.2	2.9	2.1	5.1	4.1
Headquarters Office										
OA —headquarters office	7.1	4.1	2.0	2.9	2.0	5.0	.2	17.5	4.4	5.0
General Office										
EA —general office	14.9	9.6	13.2	8.1	6.3	13.2	16.4	18.5	14.2	12.7
Transportation										
RA —railroad uses	.3	.1	.1	.2*	a	.1	.1	.1	a	.1
RB —bus uses	a	.7	.8	.8	.7	.2	.2	.2	—	.4
RC —air transport	a	.2	.2	.3	.2	.1	.1	.4	.1	.2
RD —trucking	a	—	—	—	—	.2	—	—	.1	.1
R —totals	.6	1.0	1.1	1.3	1.0	.6	.4	.7	.2	.8
Parking										
PA —customer parking	.8	.2	.5	1.0	.4	.3	.3	1.0	.1	.5
PB —commercial parking	7.9	7.6	7.3	5.0	4.9	8.8	6.2	5.1	5.5	6.5
P —totals	8.7	7.8	7.8	6.0	5.3	9.1	6.5	6.1	5.6	7.0

SERVICE—FINANCIAL—OFFICE USES

	NON-CENTRAL BUSINESS USES									
Transient Residence										
LA —hotels and other transient lodging	10.5	9.4	13.3	17.0	17.5	7.8	11.8	12.4	5.3	11.7
Residential										
DA —permanent dwelling units	1.8	1.8	2.4	1.9	6.8	4.9	1.8	2.8	6.8	3.4
Public and Organizational										
GA —public buildings	9.5	12.3	8.8	7.1	9.8	9.4	4.2	5.3	9.7	8.5
GB —organizational and charitable institutions	4.6	2.5	1.3	2.0	3.8	0.8	2.9	5.1	5.1	3.1
G —totals	14.1	14.8	10.1	9.1	13.6	10.2	7.1	10.4	14.8	11.6
Industrial										
IA —industries	2.4	.6	.5	a	.6	3.6	1.4	.5	4.2	1.5
Wholesale with Stocks										
WA—wholesale with stocks	2.1	2.9	1.5	0.5	1.1	3.7	0.9	1.0	2.6	1.8
Vacancy										
XA—vacant building or store	5.9	6.6	2.9	3.2	4.2	3.6	8.1	2.0	3.3	4.4
XB—vacant lot	.6	1.2	.6	.6	.5	.6	.2	.4	.4	.6
XC —commercial storage	.2	1.6	—	1.9	.1	.4	—	.4	—	.5
X —totals	6.7	9.4	3.5	5.7	4.8	4.6	8.3	2.8	3.7	5.5

a Less than 0.1 per cent.

* Land occupied by tracks was not measured.

For each city, 100 per cent is total floor space in the CBD, defined in the study as the ground-floor area of all blocks that lay inside the boundaries of the CBD minus alleys and plus the areas of all upper floors. A dash indicates that no value was recorded. (Based on field work and office calculations in 1952–1953 as reported by Murphy, Vance, and Epstein in *Central Business District Studies*, Worcester, Mass., 1955.)

CBD Bibliography

Bohnert, J. E., and Mattingly, Paul F. "The Delimitation of the CBD Through Time." *Economic Geography* 40 (1964): 337–347.

Bourne, L. S. "Comments on the Transition Zone Concept." *The Professional Geographer* 20 (1968): 313–316.

Bowden, Martyn J. "Downtown Through Time: Delimitation, Expansion, and Internal Growth," *Economic Geography* 47 (1971): 121–135.

Boyce, Ronald R., and Clark, W. A. V. "Selected Spatial Variable and Central Business District Sales." *Proceedings of the Regional Science Association* 11 (1963): 167–193.

Breese, Gerald W. *The Daytime Population of the Central Business District of Chicago with Particular Reference to the Factor of Transportation.* Chicago: University of Chicago Press, 1949.

Carter, H., and Rowley, G. "The Morphology of the Central Business District of Cardiff." *Institute of British Geographers, Transactions,* no. 38 (1966), pp. 119–134.

Davies, D. Hywel. "Boundary Study as a Tool in CBD Analysis: An Interpretation of Certain Aspects of the Boundary of Cape Town's Central Business District." *Economic Geography* 35 (1959): 322–345.

Davies, D. Hywel. "The Hard Core of Cape Town's Central Business District: An Attempt at Delimitation," *Economic Geography* 36 (1960): 53–69.

Davies, D. Hywel. *Land Use in Central Cape Town: A Study in Urban Geography.* Cape Town: Longmans, 1965.

Davies, R. J., and Rajah, D. S. "The Durban CBD: Boundary Delimitation and Racial Dualism" *The South African Geographical Journal* 47 (December 1965): 45–58.

de Blij, Harm J. "The Functional Structure and Central Business District of Lourenço Marques, Mocambique." *Economic Geography* 38 (1962): 56–77.

Diamond, D. R. "The Central Business District of Glasgow." Proceedings of the IGU Symposium in Urban Geography, Lund, 1960, *Lund Studies in Human Geography,* series B, *Human Geography,* no. 24 (1962), 525–534.

Foley, Donald L. "The Daily Movement of Population into Central Business Districts." *American Sociological Review* 17 (October 1952): 538–543; and "Urban Daytime Population: A Field for Demographic-Ecological Analysis." *Social Forces* 33 (1954): 323–330.

Foley, Donald L. *The Suburbanization of Administrative Offices in the San Francisco Bay Area.* Research Report 10, Real Estate Research Program, Bureau of Business and Economic Research, Berkeley: University of California, 1957.

Foley, Donald L., and Breese, Gerald. "The Standardization of Data Showing Population Movement into Central Business Districts." *Land Economics* 27 (1951): 348–353.

Griffin, Donald W., and Preston, Richard E. "Land Use in the Central Commercial Area." *Journal of Geography* 67 (1968): 342–351.

Griffin, Donald W., and Preston, Richard E. "A Reply to 'Comments on the Transition Zone Concept." *The Professional Geographer* 21 (1969): 232–237.

Griffin, Donald W., and Preston, Richard E. "A Restatement of the 'Transition Zone' Concept." *Annals of the Association of American Geographers* 56 (1966): 339–350.

Hartman, George W. "Central Business District, A Study in Urban Geography." *Economic Geography* 26 (1950): 237–244.

Hautamäki, Lauri, and Siirilä, Seppo. "Delimiting the CBD in Finland." *Fennia* 99, no. 4 (1969): 1–40.

Horwood, Edgar M., and Boyce, Ronald R. *Studies of the Central Business District and Urban Freeway Development.* Seattle: University of Washington Press, 1959.

Huhtanen, Robert J.; Mika, Paul J.; Preston, Richard E.; and Murphy, Raymond E.: *A Study of the Effects of Freeways on Central Business Districts.* Report Submitted to U.S. Department of Commerce, Bureau of Public Roads, February, 1961.

Johnson, Earl S. *The Natural History of the Central Business District with Particular Reference to Chicago.* Chicago: University of Chicago Ph.D. Dissertation, 1941. Available in microfilm.

Jonassen, C. T. *Downtown Versus Suburban Shopping: Measurement of Consumer Practices and Attitudes in Columbus, Ohio.* Columbus: The Ohio State University, Bureau of Business Research, 1953.

Jonassen, C. T. *The Shopping Center Versus Downtown: A Motivation Research on Shopping Habits and Attitudes in Three Cities.* Columbus: The Ohio State University, Bureau of Business Research, 1955.

Majid, Rosie. "The CBD of Dacca: Delimitation and Internal Structure." *Oriental Geographer* 14, no. 1 (1970): 44–63.

Mattingly, Paul F. "Delimitation and Movement of CBD Boundaries Through Time: the Harrisburg Example." *The Professional Geographer* 16, no. 6 (1964): 9–13.

Murphy, Peter E. "A Temporal Study of the Spatial Adjustment of a CBD in Terms of Central Place Principles." *Tijdschrift voor Economische en Sociale Geografie* 61, no. 1 (1970): 16–21.

Murphy, Raymond E. "Central Business District Research." Proceedings of the IGU Symposium in Urban Geography, Lund, 1960, *Lund Studies in Human Geography,* series B, *Human Geography,* no. 24 (1962), 525–534.

Murphy, Raymond E., and Vance, J. E., Jr. "A Comparative Study of Nine Central Business Districts." *Economic Geography* 30 (1954): 301–336.

Murphy, Raymond E., and Vance, J. E., Jr. "Delimiting the CBD." *Economic Geography* 30 (1954): 189–222.

Murphy, Raymond E.; Vance, J. E., Jr.; and Epstein, Bart J. *Central Business District Studies.* Reprints from *Economic Geography* with additions. Worcester, Mass.: Clark University, 1955.

Murphy, Raymond E.; Vance, J. E., Jr.; and Epstein, Bart J. "Internal Structure of the CBD." *Economic Geography* 31 (1955): 21–46.

Parkins, A. E. "Profiles of the Retail Business Section of Nashville, Tennessee." *Annals of the Association of American Geographers* 20 (1931): 164–176.

Philadelphia City Planning Commission. *Philadelphia Central District Study* (prepared by Alderson and Sessions, Philadelphia, 1951).

Preston, Richard E. "Freeway Impact on the Central Business District: the Case of Long Beach." *California Geographer* 4 (1963): 9–17.

Preston, Richard E. "Transition Zone Structure: The three-sector hypothesis." *Town Planning Review* 39, no. 3 (October 1968): 235–250.

Preston, Richard E. "The Zone in Transition: A Study of Urban Land Use Patterns." *Economic Geography* 42 (1966): 236–260.

Rannells, John. *The Core of the City: A Pilot Study of Changing Land Uses in Central Business Districts.* New York: Columbia University Press, 1956.

Ratcliff, Richard U. *The Madison Central Business Area.* Wisconsin Commerce Papers, vol. 1, no. 5. Madison: Bureau of Business Research and Service, University of Wisconsin, 1953.

Reynolds, Robert B. "Retail Specialization of Central Business Districts." *Journal of American Institute of Planners* 26, no. 4 (November 1960): 313–316.

Rowley, Gwyn. "A Note on Central Business District Research in Britain." *Professional Geographer* 17, no. 6 (November 1965): 15–16.

Russwurm, Lorne H.: "The Central Business District Retail Sales Mix, 1948–1958," *Annals of the Association of American Geographers* 54 (1964): 524–536.

Scott, Peter. "The Australian CBD." *Economic Geography* 35, no. 4 (1959): 290–314.

U.S. Bureau of the Census. *Intra-City Business Census Statistics for Philadelphia, Pa.* Prepared under supervision of Malcolm J. Proudfoot, Research Geographers. May, 1937.

U.S. Bureau of the Census. *Major Retail Centers in Standard Metropolitan Statistical Areas* (for each state), 1963 and 1967.

University of Amsterdam. *Urban Core and Inner City.* Proceedings of the International Study Week, Amsterdam, September 11–16, 1966. Leiden: Brill, 1967.

Ward, David. "The Industrial Revolution and the Emergence of Boston's Central Business District." *Economic Geography* 42 (1966): 152–171.

Weaver, David C. "Changes in the Morphology of Three American Central Business Districts 1952–1966." *Professional Geographer* 21 (1969): 406–410.

Weiss, Shirley F. *The Central Business District in Transition.* Research Paper no. 1, City and Regional Planning Studies. Chapel Hill: Department of City and Regional Planning, University of North Carolina, 1957.

Young, B. S. "Aspects of the Central Business District of Port Elizabeth, Cape Province." *Journal for Social Research* 12 (1961): pp. 27–48.

Index